NOTION SICK

VOL. 1

- Philocuriousity
- Reflection
- Notion Sickness
- Discovery
- Understanding

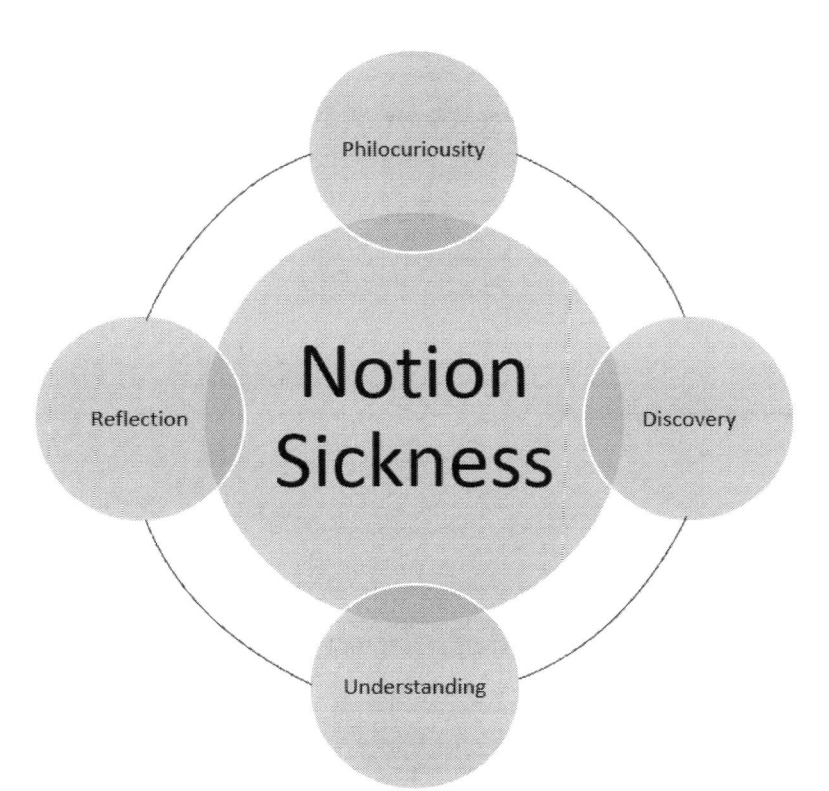

Pause to prepare…

NOTION SICK

VOL. 1

Anthology of Concepts
for the Philocurious Mind

by

Hans Dodoo

NOTION SICK | vol.1

Copyright © 2023 by Hans Dodoo

All rights reserved.

Dedicated to:

Philip Lamin
18.11.96 - 05.02.13

David Adjei
21.09.92 - 01.11.22

CONTENTS

0 – Preface – Philocuriosity at Play...................1
1 – Death with a side of Friendship...................7
2 – Time Starts Now.....................................13
3 – Last Day as A Kid..................................18
4 – What do you see?...................................22
5 – Observatory...26
6 – Pain, pain, go away................................28
7 – The Lens..31
8 – The Freedom-Discipline Paradox..............37
9 – A Penny for Your Take............................42
10 – Opportunity..47
11 – Another Opportunity.............................50
12 – Useless Lessons...................................52
13 – Eyes of Assumption...............................53
14 – Communicating in Metaphors.................55
15 – Misunderstood.....................................62
16 – The Best Chapter Ever..........................66
17 – Self-actualization.................................69
18 – Super Set..74
19 – Stream of Consciousness.......................79
20 – Collage of God....................................87
21 – Son of Man..100
22 – Flashback..104
23 – Quarter Life Learnings.........................107
24 – Notion Sick: Drink for Thought..............114
Epilogue..118
Appendix...120

0 - Preface

Philocuriousity at Play

Notion sickness is mildly experienced by many and extremely experienced by a handful. It is the sensation that arises from travelling through a universe of thoughts, ideas, and notions - whatever that sensation translates to is distinctively subjective. Notion sickness can be identified as a consequence of this journey of thoughts, whilst philocuriosity can be likened to both a psychological state or personal value **(see Appendix 2).**
Anyone who is curious about life and has a sense of intrigue concerning how much there is to know about: themselves, the world, and everything in or out of it, is philocurious. It is an alchemy of prose and poetry. What already is, and what could be.

Philocuriousity is an affinity to learn, and its process demands quality in thought. Creating quality in thought requires: Time, Space and Cause or Reason. This forms the thought quality triangle. All the sides of the triangle are equally important. If any side of the triangle were to disappear, then the 'quality thought' could evaporate either in part or in full, or may not even be formed at all (see figures 1 and 2). Quality 'in' Thought speaks to the process responsible for the resulting quality idea or outcome, rather than focusing first on the produced result (Quality 'of' Thought).

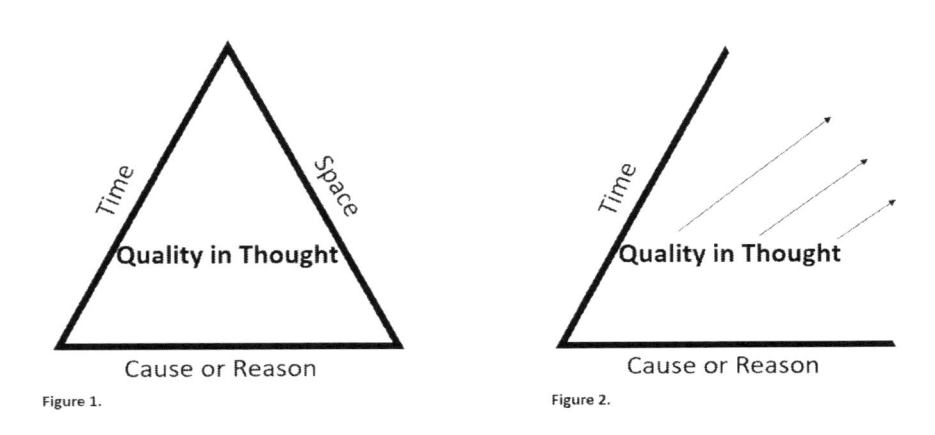

```
         /\                              /|
        /  \                            / |
       /    \                          /  |  ↗
      /Time  \Space                   /Time   ↗
     /        \                      /    |  ↗
    /Quality in Thought\            /Quality in Thought
   /          \                    /      |
  /_____\                  /_____|
   Cause or Reason                 Cause or Reason
Figure 1.                        Figure 2.
```

Time represents the amount of uninterrupted minutes, hours or days you have to ruminate or remain in a pensive state, without another activity contending for immediate priority. Space symbolises both a physical or mental space which is accessible, personal, safe, secure, spacious enough and free of clutter or distraction from things or people. Without the right boundaries, mental space is easily invaded by ruinous input. Cause or Reason simply refers to the spark or stimulus that precipitates intentional thought. It gives purpose to the thought and can be triggered by a problem, a solution, a goal, or pure curiosity.

It's easy for days, weeks and months to pass, floating through life and going through the motions without dwelling in any meaningful or quality thought. This is a critical condition; a life-threatening one because you cannot truly live unless you can truly think. Thinking is essential for living, just as breathing is for living.

This is a book about some of my thoughts, and in another chapter of my life will come a book about my story, but for now I do not yet have a full enough picture of all the pages.

Everything we know now, had to once be written about. It is perhaps the most significant and transcendent medians for human expression. Truly understanding the ideas communicated from a piece of writing or drawing is equivalent to telepathy - if telepathy were possible.

Writing (besides being a form of expression, art, logging important information or recording history), is also one of the ways we can teach ourselves and explore introspection. I thought about a concept akin to an iceberg theory, until I learned the 'Iceberg theory' already described a literary technique. Nonetheless, the comparison between our conscious and subconscious mind with an iceberg, is widely accepted. There is so much information that we retain on a daily basis which is unbeknownst to us even though it's within us. Countless connections have been processed and stored by our brains which are stored so far down our sub-consciousness we can't always recall them. Perhaps this is how déjà vu occurs. It is also known that all the faces seen in your dreams have been faces you've seen before in real life, whether you recognise them or not. Your brain can't invent new faces, but it can throw up old ones it's seen but never recalled. Such an experience feels new even though it's not, meaning we already have so much within us that we can teach or re-teach ourselves or others as 'new' information. All of which can be unearthed through writing. Writing is a versatile tool and can be used as the shovel, the rope, the anchor, the saw, the hammer, the screwdriver or even the pillow. It can also make a satisfying meal - providing some food for thought.

I can accept the fact that this particular compilation will be several lengths from perfect. The attempt to capture and distil some of my more specific thoughts and ideas into a jar that can be sealed and later consumed by another, cannot be a perfect procedure. But it can produce a potent outcome, with and by the right perspective.

Perspective is the key ingredient that fuels effective mentorship. A well sculpted piece can be modelled on another well sculpted piece – and so on. Your perspective and interpretations become your original contribution to the world. Moulding a thorough perspective means taking the special, unique, and creative ways in which someone else (through their own experience), sees things, and consolidating it with your own current perspective to generate a new, unique sum. It's an unrivalled method for inspiring great thinking. It opens up a whole world of tools and learnings through expansive multi-varied, critical thinking. There isn't one method of mentoring. As much as there exists primary mentorship - through real interaction with someone, you can also receive secondary mentorship through the words you read and study, the voice you listen to, or actions you watch. So, choose your primary and secondary mentors wisely. Mentorship should always be a relationship and process that emphasises guided discovery from mentor to mentee, rather than an enforcement of ideas and self. "Good coaches teach you how to think and arm you with the fundamental tools necessary to execute properly" - Kobe Bryant.

Reading encourages me to keep an open mind, which is vital, because not all things are what they seem. I've learnt this cliché truth in many unusual ways - one of which is through introverted people. It is a missed opportunity to completely ignore an introvert when they don't engage in a standard way or in social environments. Instead, pay attention to them and engage with them in the way they most prefer. There may be an urge and desire for them to connect with others, but just not necessarily through conventional means or in social environments. This doesn't mean they should be ignored. Rather, this urge inspires discrete innovation. Introverts, alternatively, are capable of building the most ingenious bridges for connecting with other people, which end up sometimes being a medium used by many others. They may also have something significant to share without making much noise about it. However, much of this could be easily missed if you overlook the subtleties and only pay attention to the obvious.

Some entries will be louder than others (for different individuals). Regardless, don't ignore what is immediately loud, and at the same time, be inquisitive about the things that are also quiet. In the spirit of philocuriousity, the following passages should leave you with either more or just as many questions as potential answers.

Pause to ponder…

1 - Death with a side of Friendship

Death is imminent. Numbering your days, or in other words, being aware of your mortality is a display of wisdom. It's a state of mind which forces you to prioritise your focus and affairs. It's a posture which lends you at least some room, to put your house in order - lest you be caught off guard by finality.

Death's promise isn't some abstract advert, applicable first to other humans and then eventually to us at some stage. Its primary target audience is us, now. Yet still, both the potency and imminence of its inevitable actuality, is shielded by a thick armour of subconscious narcissism which guards the ego. It remains that way, and the ego grows having swallowed humility whole (oftentimes without the awareness of the conscience) and likely wisdom along with it, until this armour is penetrated, either by a profound near-death experience or by death knocking on your own door, but for someone else. Someone close, and if not close, then at least important in your world and for your world. When that layer of armour is pierced the ego is compromised, confronted and fragile. The consequence may be a damaged ego for a period of time, until the armour of narcissism is re-patched, and ego rebuilt. Alternately, that damage may be permanent, left unrepaired and armour unrestored. For creatures commonly at the mercy of mortality, we parade in technicolour dream coats of immortality and wield paper swords of pride without any real shield.

No one is too important to die. This force is no respecter of person. We know this through experience but don't admit it on paper. Some people are immortal on paper. It can be argued that the more important and celebrated a person is, or the more they have to contribute, the more aware of death they should be - as well as humbled by that awareness. Others who look to them should also subscribe to that outlook and attitude. Instead, perspectives are distorted, and vision remains myopic, in a way which allows for these individuals to become immortalised both in mind and in culture.

You can survive the unthinkable; only to be taken out by the mundane. There's no pattern or forecast. Therefore, it is a very precarious approach to withhold your idea from the world for any longer than as soon as practically possible. It is a matter of urgency. You should and must express and communicate what it means to be you before you leave, otherwise you rubbish your reason for being. This expression is imperative for the sake of yourself and others, including those who will come after.

Every accomplishment gained or pursued which is unattached to a sense of fulfilment remains dull and drained of colour in the face of a life lost. Futility should never be the sum of a life. Unfortunately, it often dominates the equation. It's a sad truth that most people never wake up, even after a wakeup call. A modicum of morbid thought about yourself or a loved one should be enough injection to concentrate your priorities. Maybe it's a good idea to prioritise or re-prioritise, even before death attempts to do so on our behalf.

What actually matters and holds the most significance next to investing in family, is the intentional shared journey and dual effort in building, sustaining and protecting a friendship, to a degree or measure that transcends the common understanding of the word. The relationship of a friendship is one that is majorly emblematic of deep philosophical fundamentals. There's a mirror wedged between these two abstracts which clearly reflects the same properties, especially in their linguistic association.

The English translation of the Greek word philosophy means 'love of wisdom', and encapsulates infinite existential intricacies such as meaning, time, consciousness, knowledge, ethics, relationships, reality, and everything in between. The word philo (love) embodies both the noun and the verb in the same, emphasising both a deep affection for, and intense commitment to - in the same cementing and consolidating vein as a marriage. It captures in its meaning, a connection to, association with and affinity for, all in one. 'Philia' is distinguished in ancient Greek as one out of the four main types of love and the one which represents the idea of friendship. Such a specific and unique kind of love is characterised by the organic mechanics of the relation between two individuals - determined in part by nature and culture, and in part by the pair of them. It captures and establishes a mutual reciprocation of expectations and attitude, both spoken and unspoken, and defines the same embodiment of doing and knowing love in the same.

Such information suggests that the terms 'friend' or 'friendship' should not be so ordinarily and carelessly tossed around, but rather should represent a kind of compelling, symbolic and sacred pilgrimage, similar to how we see love. When this happens as it should, 'friend' becomes 'loved one'.

An authentic connection is seldom come-by, and not easily cultivated. Alongside honesty, one of my main personal measures of the strength or type of bond I share with someone, is the part of my being from which my laughter yearns when relating with them. It's an indicator that can't be forged. A special form of communication and understanding that is priceless, invaluable, and somewhat irreplaceable. The laughter you share with a specific person (although may sound the exact same to the ears), carries a unique fingerprint and DNA only attached to that relationship. It comes from a certain place that can't be replicated in the same way. That laughter is the highest gift. Which is why losing a friend is fatal. It is unfortunate for young people especially, to know death so tangibly, yet still, it is every individual's responsibility to become well acquainted with its realness.

It's never real until it is. But when it is, you're hit by a hurricane of anguish; doomed by a natural disaster, wrecked on a lonely island. The world is bleak and you're inconsolable. All the combinations of condolences and apologies under the sun have been uttered a thousand times and sound like nothing more than a custom or formality. The sounds of consolation echo emptily. You know they might genuinely mean what they say, and the gesture is appreciated, but there is nothing they can do - or you can do. How can a big elephant in a small room be so elusive. There is a sense of it ultimately being your problem to confront. So eventually, you crawl gradually, then limp from your own 'surreality' and only partly into the communal reality - with half yourself stuck on either side. Here, you begin dressing in diplomacy and prepare to complete the transition into the 'real' world, still with everlasting ties to the other. From now on we are conscious of the deficit that remains, regardless of the surplus gained. There is a specific piece gone, and so the pain stays. It just turns from a sharp pain into a dull ache, and you get somewhat used to living with it. You pay to remorse what you loaned from pride and procrastination. You plead with hopelessness for a little more time, but its bailiffs are relentless; so you offer instalments of what you can in the meantime. You regret how many times you didn't express your love. You sleep with one eye open in case it ever happens again, knowing it will and eventually, it does.

One day death will have to take a day off.

This life could actually be the best. It was nearly the best, but it wasn't. I'm now sure that, that's the point. It wasn't meant to be. It's not the final stop.
Glimpses of euphoria and dystopia, compose a tormenting tease.
On the other hand, this life could be catastrophic. It was nearly the

worst, but it wasn't. I'm now sure it wasn't meant to be. It's not a damnation, it's the human dichotomy.

2 - Time Starts Now

Our own sand timers were turned for us. We had no awareness. We weren't ready, we weren't set. At some point we just realised we were on a timer. Still, this innocence is no excuse to be oblivious to the sand that falls through the hourglass. A checkpoint such as this one, is where we recognize that enough sand has passed through the hourglass of our life for us to be able to see clearer through it. We finally realise we want to take ownership of our hourglass and we *need* to take ownership of our hourglass. By that time, we're a quarter way through. That's if you're fortunate enough or attentive enough to realise it then. The truth is that we only start trying to live when we realise there's a timer, because the moment you realise there's a timer is the real start of your search for purpose.

Many people don't even realise the turn of the hourglass and therefore are never fuelled by a sense of end. Our own mortality is an abstract concept to us. On the other hand, the trigger for some people's realisation or epiphany of this timer, is a sudden awareness sparked by a particular event and characterised by Maslow's hierarchy of needs. This lightbulb moment is fuelled by a search for self-actualization, purpose and meaning. All this alerts us to the fact that we have a time constraint. One that is set for us to accomplish our life's purpose.

The momentum of time is infinitely compounded. It pulls with it all of life and everything in it. Therefore, it is wise to use this momentum to our advantage by compounding our proactivity along with it - which will inevitably lead to multiplied productivity. It is, however, unwise to sit still in the face of such a colossal force. It will have no mercy.

If not one extra second on the clock is ever guaranteed, why do we carry around bags of hubris and entitlement, enough for tomorrow and many days after that. Perhaps a partial reason for this is that eternity is ingrained in our souls. Even so, we still have zero say or control over how much time we have on earth. Whilst we are incessantly caged by time in its linear, chronological form, there remain other variations of it which we know of but cannot experience at present. For example: boundless time, historical time, and psychological time (the way other individuals perceive and relate to time). The vastness and uniqueness of time, and the fact that it has no identical synonym, should fuel our respect for it and inspire an attempt to exchange with it more creatively. This can be done through tracing and transcending it with things that stand the test of time such as: music, art, culture, agriculture, photos, sculpting, writing.

Time is the real currency, this is the reason why in its basic form, it is spent accordingly. I'm of the belief that part of our time must be spent helping others. Nevertheless, it is up to each individual how they divide their capital. What remains important is your awareness and consciousness of time and how much is being spent, where, and on what.

Just like money, time should not be squandered or wasted, and it should be every person's moral responsibility to spend some of what is his in acts of kindness - for the benefit of others. This gives purpose or meaning to that person's currency in more ways than when compared with expenditure on other miscellaneous activity. What good is spending all your money on useless junk? It is as good as not spending it at all. The same is with time. We are stewards of the portion that is given to us. If we use it well, its ripple effect will multiply.

When you decide to give away time out of love or care, do so in a way that actually adds value to others when subtracting it from yourself; because either way, it will still be deducted from you, but may not necessarily always add to others. Make sure it is not wasted or meaningless when shared. The expense of that time must be exchanged for value or create value that is timeless and surpasses time itself in such a way that the more people you share it with, the greater it will become.

It is a paradox that for one to experience life fully they must also spend time on things they are unsure of or have a bad impression of. Indeed, exploring new things isn't wrong. The fault lies in doing so blindly, ignorantly, or simply following the crowd. I learned from a mentor to account for time in the same way as money - save some, invest some and spend some. This is a prudent ideology which is open to personal interpretation and adoption.

The first way to maximise time is to eliminate confusion. It is the adversary of all progress.
Confusion resembles a bunch of tangled cables. The feelings evoked in its midst are akin to helplessness. You don't immediately know where to start from or what the root cause is. It very much looks like an impossible task to tackle before you even start. You rather, just want a fresh set of untangled cables; and so, your first instinct is to attempt pulling apart this entanglement forcefully, rather than giving attention to it one cable at a time. Sometimes even the sheer appearance of complexity can turn us from attempting at all.

The natural, involuntary remedy to confusion is to ask questions, just as coughing is a natural, involuntary remedy to a disturbed throat. Suppressing or discouraging questions in any way can be rather damaging and crippling, because it feels like the subduing of a natural instinct. Furthermore, the urge to question must be well directed. It must be controlled, calculated, and considered in order to be effective - otherwise it becomes futile in addressing confusion.

Confusion is a king constraint, and a thief of time in any context. Therefore, being equipped with good questions is a way of anticipating and preventing its intrusion. The more you ask the right questions the more likely you are to learn and weaken the potential grip of confusion. The right question is like the one untangled cable that frees up a few more of the tangled cables.

3 - Last Day as A Kid

It's a strange thought trying to recall the exact age, date, time, or place I crossed over from boyhood into manhood. There was no moment. I just seemed to become increasingly conscious of the gradual transition. Even my awareness was unsure. Am I there yet? Is this it? I think I'm kind of here. We tend not to realise how elusive transitions are. We just arrive at certain destinations without registering the journey we've just been on. There are so many periods in time we don't notice have started or ended.

A good friend of mine brought to my attention a mind tickling, oddly irritating thought that still pokes at me. "There was a particular day that was the last day we played out as kids in our neighbourhood, but when exactly was that day? do we even remember it?" It's unlikely we do. The fact is, we were so oblivious to knowing that the last day we ever played out with our friends as kids in our area, was actually going to be our last day doing so. Perhaps we can singularly distinguish that day as the last day we were kids.

How interesting would it be if we could recall the exact eyes in which we previously saw the world through, in the same way we recall a memory or feeling? It is a phenomenon, the way in which children and adults see the same world and situations so differently. There must be a perfect optimum somewhere in the middle. Children are yet to develop the same type of filter adults have, and therefore arguably see the world for what it really is. Logic and learnt principles could almost be an inapparent blocker.

Childhood is an extremely special period, which you only discover was precious after it's behind you, or just about to be. "What's the first thing you think when I say 'childhood'?" - a random text message I received from a friend on 09/02/2021.
My reply, "Confused. Why does our perception of life get to be shaped most when we know the least?".

Our way of thinking and how we receive information is largely formed in our childhood.
All of us go through early life experiences (whether they be traumatic or positive) that shape us and our perception, and thus, determine how we view and process our adult experiences. Although the emotions, thoughts and feelings belonging to the perspective of this early period may demand to have their way, a large proportion of us try to resist most of our 'childish' tendencies or opinions, due to existing social mechanisms which are assimilated as we grow. This phase of so called 'maturing', is also riddled with increasingly new social or existential information for us to absorb. On the other hand, a small proportion of people don't psychologically outgrow that early childhood period. It is not because they purposely flout social norms, but rather because they are stuck in replay of a previous scene within their life's story. Whether this happens consciously or subconsciously their film won't play past this part, and they stay stuck in that scene.

They are frozen in time and don't even realise it. They fail to recognise or acknowledge that they haven't grown.

Our learning naturally continues from childhood as we age, and informs our perception. It could be argued that we should completely abandon and rubbish a portion of the learnings we picked up as children just because we are adults who now 'know better'. However, knowing better doesn't mean what you once knew was necessarily wrong, it just means you now have more perspective. Even so, with little life experience, children can sometimes ask the most profound questions which illuminate the path towards greater enlightenment. They're also adept at making friends, building bonds and shedding inhibition. Embracing the contrasts between a child-like interpretation and a mature mindset can further increase the dynamism of an otherwise parochial perspective. If wisdom is the correct application of knowledge, wouldn't it be wise to also effectively apply your childhood knowledge and perception alongside your adult one, to give you a more rounded, wiser outlook?

The wisest of people (a seemingly exclusive calling), compile the knowledge they've acquired at all stages of their life and utilise it situationally and contextually. They choose when to apply a childlike perception, when to employ the grown-up filter, and when to leverage their experience of that very transitional spectrum - especially in addressing uncertainty. If knowledge is power, wisdom is authority.

The trajectory of one's life is significantly influenced as a child and even more so during this distinct and significant transitional spectrum called adolescence. Youth presents a plethora of options, combinations, complexities, uncertainties, and possibilities. The more definitive decisions you begin to make as you grow, nullify these. An adult's habits, beliefs and outlook are strongly shaped from when they're quarter aged and beyond, through both their consciousness and subconsciousness. This becomes the framework and nucleus by which they navigate the rest of their lives. Pay attention to every belief you accept or dismiss, as well as the behaviours you cultivate.

The older you get the more variables are cemented, patterns established, and the less unpredictable the trend of your life is. Although the possibility of opportunities still exists, unchanging patterns and biases guarantee the same outcomes. It is a contributing factor to why dreams and aspirations become but only a puff of smoke for a lot of 'grown-ups'. You may even begin to seek the opposite of opportunity as you age; perhaps not as explicitly as it sounds, but by becoming more risk averse and inclining towards predictability, stability, and 'certainty'.

4 - What do you see?

"Life moves pretty fast, if you don't stop and look around once in a while, you could miss it" - Ferris Bueller.

Observation exercised properly is mind blowing. Such a tool as this is multi-dimensional. It's a vehicle for transporting and transcending. Sight is a sharp and agile sense. You can change the focus of observation from one thing to the other in the blink of an eye and with the instinct of the peripheral. This happens just as easily as a new thought springs from a previous one, and several spirals of thought originate from one inception. Meaningful observation and good discernment are tethered to each other, as a balloon is to a string, or an investment to expectation. Good discernment knows what to observe, and how to interpret the observation.

Some common mistakes easily made when observing include: only paying attention to what's entertaining or comfortable to watch, whilst ignoring what is hard to look at; being easily impressionable; imitating superficial trends; mimicking the wrong behaviours; making bad assumptions; and maintaining a confirmation bias. Such habits perpetuated can send you into a negative feedback loop, robbing you of the full truth and the meaning behind the painting. Long term recurrence of this pattern will build around you, a false reality which you become one with. This will ultimately break you when the painting is shattered by the timely, accurate, merciless strike of truth. Or worse yet, you become immune to the truth.

The primary reason why we fail to observe as we should, is simply because we don't know what exactly to observe, why we are doing so and how to do so purposefully; how to connect meaning rather than construct it, and how to be ok with not identifying or knowing certain meanings. It is a tool that must be sharpened constantly by using it. For our observations to mean anything, we must first acknowledge them, before sorting them into different arrangements of meaning and truth - which may or may not be interconnected. Observation is costly because we pay in time, thought, attention and other existential resources. Unfortunately, the cost is either too high or the purchase is too irrelevant for most. In modern times, where the scenes of life are played at x2 speed; only few have the patience to play at x1 let alone x0.5. Any time spent defrosting or slow cooking food for thought feels like a drag - a waste of time. And for intentional observation seems the same.

Rich observation is enough to stir up and stimulate the soul. It helps to identify the values behind both tangible and intangible things. It's both liberating and depressing to realise that many things don't mean much. Many things we glorify don't hold much pure, intrinsic value at all. Observing what is really important distinguishes this truth amidst the blurriness of materialism.

Since we all place value on owning possessions that no one else has, why don't we take pride in our uniqueness; our fingerprint; our perspective. Instead, we all choose to see and think the same. We'd rather have different shoes than different ideas. Not to say we won't have any varied ideas, but most of us would be more concerned if the person next to us was wearing the same thing on their feet, than if they were thinking the same thoughts and ideas. We're happy to all think the same and contribute the same duplicated perspective to the world. It's acceptable (perhaps encouraged) to emphasise uniqueness in your appearance; and care about looking or presenting distinctly from the person on your left. However, the issue exists when we place utmost priority on this over differentiating the way we think or see. Nevertheless, some are incapable of either - they let the herd dress them physically and feed them mentally. You've probably heard this one before but if 99% of people had a Porsche, a Porsche's value would mean nothing. In the same way when 99% of us have the same essence to offer mentally, philosophically, and physically; meaning and insight become near impossible to discover and 1% are left to pioneer the way for innovation and enlightenment.

There is nothing under the sun that isn't worth deeply observing. There will be a real meaning behind most things - and a story associated. Time can never be deemed wasted by observing these things, unless they push one further away from learning something new. Even just reinforcing certain old lessons is at times necessary.

Listening is also a form of observation. Combined with a sufficient measure of patience and pensiveness, it births discovery. The greatest problem solvers knew this. It's for that same reason Albert Einstein's solution to saving the world in its proposed final hour of doom, would be to 'spend 59 minutes thinking about the problem', and 'one minute solving it' - how better to think about or define the problem than to observe it thoroughly.

5 - Observatory

Well executed mental architecture is required for designing a personal, secluded space in the fortress of your mind which will be an observatory. This will add value to your fortress. It will be built in the nucleus of your mind's eye, mounted with a lens telescope interchangeable between hindsight and foresight. A gallery of memories and thoughts, a lab for careful processing and analysis of life's phenomena.

This place is a thing of beauty. It's the window to the gallery of life. It is where new images or ideas are spotted, captured, processed then hung on display, and lessons are shelved just as books in a library, ready for when they are needed again. If ever. The **useless lessons** gather dust. But the vivid ones catch our eye regardless of whether we choose to open them or not. Pay attention to this room, this space. Visit regularly. Clean and maintain it. Share it. Invite a close friend or loved one into it occasionally - but respect the space, as it's not a lounge. Date all your collections and observations; keep a big visible clock in there so you can keep track of time. This is important because time becomes easily elusive in there. Leave the spear key or code for at least one other person you trust to have; in the case you aren't able to come back for one reason or the other.

An observatory built wrongly, with a distorted telescope, is more dangerous the more elaborately it's built. It is, a place of privacy, but should still undergo regular auditing from a trustworthy party, who is permitted to look through that telescope in the form of an intimate and constructive exchange. Although, the majority of processing and analysis remains one's own responsibility.

The person who misjudges both the construction and maintenance of their observatory surrenders to ignorance and oblivion. Delusion is their permanent fortress. Both their false sense of shelter and everlasting prison. They'll continue to repel truth and attract untruth. Fabrication draws their reality and colours their pride. This person is doomed for good; pleased for bad. He is king of himself and king also to himself. We've all heard many stories which illustrate this type.

Avoid building a shabby observatory that houses a blurry lensed, warped telescope. With this, you cannot seek or find the truth. If an observatory is a place for spectating natural, scientific phenomena, then it should be founded upon objectivity and open mindedness; decorated with the humility of how much is unknown and to be learnt.

6 - Pain, pain, go away

Success is the legacy of pain, but so is destruction. Hardship is a great catalyst for progress, and pain can either be a stimulus to create, innovate, act, build, strengthen and strategise - or a prerequisite for shutting down. We want not to suffer the same torment or bear the same agony, so we summon all our resources and efforts to break out of it. The problem is that once we emerge from pain and find comfort, we lose the greatest stimulus we ever had - and become exposed to complacency. Human beings are built with strong cores and weak frames. On one hand, we can be very fragile and easily susceptible, and on the other hand endure the most merciless of ordeals; remaining unbroken. The strangest part about our attitude towards pain is the fact that we prefer it to boredom. This scientifically proven obscurity demonstrates why pain is such a potent and important stimulus - why it isn't solely designed to destroy us.

Pain is a dynamic experience, therefore our reaction to it must be dynamic. It is not entirely possible to prepare for the feeling that it is. However, simply trying to shrug off pain, as a panacea to its discomfort, is problematic because it encourages us to overlook the details, intricacies, and uniqueness of what makes up that pain; as well as what can be gained from it. Relying on avoidance as a coping or defence mechanism is a flawed and unsustainable strategy. Neglected issues may accumulate and eventually become too heavy to bear. The weight of this burden is so heavy that it can crush your sense of direction and hinder your understanding and success. Moreover, when you reach a point where you cannot bear the load any longer, even a minor incident could become the unexpected, final straw that breaks you.

With this in mind, our mindset towards pain should be to address each instance as it comes. How we tackle it should be tailored and dependent on 'what' it is and its severity. Dealing with every occurrence doesn't necessarily mean being pedantic, but instead, staying sensitive to the sensation and how it manifests itself, rather than brushing it under the rug. Our brain loves a shortcut, and we always want a go to, quick fix method that works for every problem. However, the more problems your mind is given to process (on top of the plethora of daily functions calculations and thoughts), the more mental shortcuts it needs to create to handle the demand. These heuristics work for a number of trivial affairs - but when the matter is as serious as pain, the reaction must be dynamic, specific, and intentional - as opposed to passive or generic.

Many who know pain learn how to compartmentalise. Perhaps because there are some types of pain that cannot be fully remediated on earth. It is locked far away in an abyss, to ensure the feeling is forgotten and never re-lived. It becomes a forbidden cave in the depths of your subconsciousness - where the myth of the boogie man lives and grows more ominous. Distractions become a regular refuge;

one that always changes its coordinates. Rather than constantly seeking refuge, seek resolution. Although the pain may not be completely curable to a full degree, it can be an essential or special propellant for the journey. This energy source is easily locked away and unharnessed when misperceived. But note (as Joseph Campbell alluded), "the cave you fear to enter holds the treasure you seek".

7 - The Lens

Perception is reality. Your lens, or the filter on them, determine the colours you will see or won't see, and the direction your feet will follow. It is of inestimable seriousness that one's lens is therefore free of distortion and consulted by critical thinking.
The condition and clarity of your lens is a matter of urgency because your perception also determines the state of your heart - which is the core of your being.

Critical thinking is inescapably imperative. Yet still, it is extremely uncommon and understated today for various reasons; one being that we're ignorant of the negative consequences attached to not practising it, as well as the corresponding consequences typically being delayed or deferred. The relationship between having a clear lens and critical thinking is founded on possessing independent patterns of thought and reflection. Furthermore, a sustained measure of introspection as well as extrospection, are a key part of developing autonomous opinions and conceptions (which may at times, look unconventional).

Unfortunately, many opt for the cheap and popular practice of impulsive, ignorant conformity. Such a subtle form of mental captivity, often results in the wrong lens being used to perceive, interpret, and understand the most urgent of issues or subjects. Conformance is the easy option in many instances, and having the mental fortitude to think for yourself is both rare and undervalued - in some cases, even ridiculed. Having a natural default of independent, critical thinking, over consensus-like thinking is a quality which is of great gravity. Even though such a habit can be challenging to cultivate, it is a matter of real and fake; truth and lie; or even life and death.

Yes, consensus driven thinking does have its use cases - such as when fleeing from imminent danger or combining efforts towards a morally compelling and positive cause. However, following the crowd blindly or with a clouded lens and lack of careful evaluation, is a treacherous route to traverse. It leads away from establishing any real personal fulfilment and self-assurance. There must be a moment of pause to ask the right questions internally (to self) and externally (to others). An action which translates as re-adjusting or cleaning your lens. It is normal for vision to occasionally become blurred. However, the real detriment lies in doing nothing about it. Nonchalance in this context is especially dangerous when another entity is directly responsible for causing the blur or obstruction to visibility. In essence, whoever controls your perception, also controls your reality.

Traditional sources of media (from newspapers to Hollywood) have previously bulk sold warped lenses which they deceptively labelled as authentic, or worse yet - essential, in a bid to control the mass' perception and inform people's life decisions. In some cases where people have refused to buy what they're selling, they've desperately resorted to forcing these lenses on people's faces through various creative ways. This scenario occurs increasingly due to fierce competition from contemporary, independent media sources. Nonetheless, amongst this war for attention and commitment, the over saturation of information becomes more extreme - especially in the arenas of social media. This makes the prospect of developing any rich and rounded perspective counterproductively more difficult. Instead, one finds themselves trudging through a thick swamp of opinions, and eventually dissolving into that swamp themselves as another added opinion.

No single perspective forms truth on its own. Rather, what does, is a combination of multiple reliable and valid sources of information - as well as the consideration of other alternative perspectives. The correct level of intelligent collaboration and constructive conflict are central ingredients in creating an innovative perception. Intelligent collaboration means combining with the right people, and doing so in the right way. Extracting enough of their point of view to see something from a different, yet trustworthy angle. This is a process that adds a highly defined, panoramic feature to your personalised lens, helping you to absorb many reliable perspectives and draw your own conclusions. Secondly, conflict acts as the product test, sanity test or test of fire for that perspective, to ensure it is valid or justifiable firstly to self, then others. This is the process of refinement for your personal lens; to ensure its clear, sturdy, and purged of any impurities. To make certain your perspective is well considered, open minded and versatile, but not easily 'tossed by every wind of doctrine'.

The lens is a constant work in progress, and it is important to enhance perspective by exercising it continuously with evaluation, adjustments, challenges, and flexibility - while at the same time remaining rooted in axiomatic truth and principles. This aids in maintaining enough open mindedness towards people and concepts - while at the same time remaining well grounded.

It's easy to make life an efficient operation, and to allow that efficiency to remain sufficient, whilst life's meaning continues to remain insufficient. Perspective adds or removes colour from certain things; selectively enriching or dulling the meaning of those things in the process. With the right lens, the unseen details evidently make up the bigger picture because they underline where God is in the detail, and how this detail is magnified in the bigger picture. Both the miniscule strokes and the larger portrait, trigger an enlightened vision and understanding which looms progressively clearer and more defined than an 8k high-definition display. This kind of epiphany happens in the same way as when an assembly of individuals collectively project the heavenly consonance of a choir, but independently are only singing a single note.

Perspective is delicate, intricate, very nuanced, and must be carefully considered as so - especially when shared with others. It can be incredibly unique to an individual, and this uniqueness is irreplaceably noteworthy. No two people can see every detail and every picture the same way at all times. This mysterious peculiarity should be captured, bottled and studied indefinitely.

Often when people don't know how to effectively communicate their perspective well, it comes across as banal, common-speak. It's difficult to capture exactly what you want or need to say when the knowledge is either very specific or tacit. Most people often have life experiences which give them a different insight or look into a few of life's mysteries, marvels, ironies, questions and constants - but don't know how to communicate it in an original or somewhat inspiring, authentic way. These experiences may not be unique in nature, but will be unique through your specific lens, and therefore will contain a specific **chuvstvo**. Nevertheless, more commonly, this ingredient is absent and what many intend for the influence, exaltation, and motivation of others; comes out with generic value-pack packaging, instead of having a real authentic brand stamped on it. Quite uncompelling and dull.

- Life's too short
- Life goes on
- Time flies
- You win some, you lose some
- Every dark cloud has a silver lining
- The grass isn't always greener
- Money doesn't buy happiness
- Life goes on (some more)
- Ignorance is bliss
- Don't judge a book by its cover
- There's plenty of fish in the sea
- Good things come to those who wait
- It is what it is

While these phrases or idioms may represent truisms and have their rightful place in our interactions - when it comes to translating a really nuanced piece of information, what you really want or need deep down, is the golden nugget explanation of why that saying is true from that person's perspective. Unfortunately, such sayings in certain contexts feel lazy, unambitious, avoidant, neglectful, and dismissive towards pursuing substance. I'm almost certain the author of Ecclesiastes could have summed up all his wonderful work as 'it is what it is', but thankfully he didn't.

8 - The Freedom – Discipline Paradox

Freedom and discipline are usually perceived as mutually exclusive. Both ideas separated are seen to have the other as a trade-off, or be attached to a similarly opposing opportunity cost. It may seem like the practice of discipline is a sacrifice of freedom and that it is necessary to neglect both discipline and its principles to gain full freedom. However, this is the paradox.

There is a major discrepancy between how freedom is romanticised, and how it's actualised. The romantic idea of freedom is infinite and without parameters or consequences. It disregards discipline as almost non-existent in its equation. In reality, we have very little knowledge of what real freedom consists of, which actually introduces limitations and unexpected consequences when we try to explore it. In reality, we are more inclined than we think, to feel the absence of discipline without realising or even admitting so. We are at the very least, subconsciously aware of the obscurity and uncertainty that possibly awaits a disorganised type of freedom.

Choosing to over-indulge in any form of hedonism for the sake of it, might seem like a liberating experience. However, the biological and psychological consequence associated with this, is the resulting entrapment that proceeds this type of unruly exchange with freedom. On the other hand, adhering very strictly to a set of principles may seem like the real trap (as it feels restrictive as opposed to freeing). Nonetheless, these two concepts don't have to be mutually exclusive. They can be intertwined into a more compelling, bespoke philosophy when they are regarded as equally necessary. Understanding how these two ideas can combine, firstly requires defining them clearly but separately, before establishing where and how they align.

Freedom is an experience. Freedom is the experience of not either being or feeling confined, trapped, imprisoned, or enslaved. It can occur both physically and psychologically.

Discipline is the act of regulating one's behaviour in a way that fits a set of principles, rules, systems, or ideals in a consistent manner. It is an act (or lack thereof), which can also take place both physically and psychologically.

Freedom is a complex concept that can be seen as an experience. By closely analysing the intricacies and mechanisms of this experience, we can gain a deeper understanding of how to affect it. Looking at the pencil sketch that represents our different encounters, we are able to dissect the different shades and combinations that make up experience. In other words, by examining the details of an experience, we can gain insights into the underlying factors that contribute to it.

An experience is a compound of feeling and occurrence which can be illustrated through the following equation defined as the **'Reverse Experience Paradigm'**:

$$\frac{\text{Perspective}}{\text{Emotion}} \times \text{Occurrence} = \text{Experience}$$

This dynamic, underlines the reverse engineering of what an experience is and its individual components. You had an experience: 1. because something happened (occurrence), 2. because you felt a certain way - a sensation that is an inevitable reaction (emotion), and 3. the way you felt or your emotion (the denominator), was influenced by your perspective. Like any complete equation, when inverted in the opposite direction it will always translate the same way, with the same respective output. Therefore, the Reverse Experience equation can be understood from various angles. Experience divided by occurrence, multiplied by emotion, can equal your perspective - meaning experiences can also define your views and outlook.

Your perspective is divided into every category of emotion that you could possibly feel. How you perceive life is the input that feeds into either of these various potential feelings; acting as a catalyst when filtered into the relevant emotion. The stimulation of emotion is inevitable. Love, joy, happiness, peace, frustration, sympathy, apathy, confusion, sorrow, hate etc. - your individual perspective is the initial influence that determines and activates any particular emotional state such as these. It is for this very reason, the same thing can be loved by one person and hated by another.

Now, if freedom is indeed an experience based on the components outlined in the Reverse Experience Paradigm, it also must be a combination of how you perceive, what you feel, and an occurrence that takes place. You may not have much control over what occurs, but through your perception and its influence on your emotion, you will have partial control over the resulting experience. If you can adapt and mould your initial perception, you will be able to alter the outcome of your experience - also in the context of freedom. You have the capacity for adjusting your perspective in a way which stimulates freedom (if given the right tools). Even when you're trapped in circumstance, you can be free in thought and experience a full result of freedom - albeit more unconventional or challenging.

Lack of discipline leads to confusion, uncertainty, lack of direction and fear (which are all further traps). If perspective is the dial within your control that can influence the total outcome of the freedom experience, then discipline is the hand that consciously turns this dial.

With the aforementioned definition of discipline in mind (adhering to a set of principles consistently) - surely if those principles align to your personal idea of freedom, as well as your core values, then technically in such a case discipline should equal freedom. So, therefore, the ultimate goal should be to discipline ourselves in complying with the same definition and standards we set for our own version of freedom and adhering to it consistently.

Firstly, for this connection to come alive, it requires each individual to actually do the work in defining a criterion of what freedom is for themselves (without relying on or adopting groupthink). It is not only possible but encouraged to set your own measure and standards of freedom - the same way you can for success. This is part of what it means to influence the Reverse Experience Paradigm; by controlling your perspective. Some of the common elements of freedom include time; options or alternatives to choose from; the ability to do, act or express independence; fulfilment etc. All of which can be somewhat impacted through discipline and perspective.

Furthermore, discipline gives you the tools to maximise your pursuit and experience of freedom. Suppose you wanted to play the piano to express yourself through music, freely, without limitation. You cannot enjoy that oh-so desired liberty of creative, euphoric, and transporting musical expression, without the hours and years of discipline learning scales. When your perspective is able to grasp the bigger picture, you will see how the two concepts marry - thus making your relationship with disciplined practice feel less like a constraint.

Nothing is gained for free, and the cost of freedom (beneath a surface level view), is discipline. This is the freedom discipline paradox.

9 - A Penny for Your Take

"I will never change my mind! I am a partisan of the truth! I will always be a partisan of the truth! I mean, how absurd is the idea of giving this breed of people (if they can even be called that), the same rights as someone of my class. They are NOT members of society and I consider it insulting that they would ever be deemed worthy enough to concern myself with. I am the rich man in his castle, and they are the poor man at his gate. That's the way God has ordered things; the highly and the lowly. Whose fault is it they're naked, without food, dirty, cold? I ask you again, whose fault, is it? Is it my fault? Is it!? I am a partisan of the truth, and the truth is NO!

Charity? Well, charity can't begin if you're homeless. You must understand that providing for everyone else subtracts from *our* wealth, and I don't want to share. I shouldn't have to sponsor laziness and incompetence, or worse, risk infection from poverty. There must be enough social and economic distance between someone of my stature and the hoi polloi. I have worked HARD to accumulate the more that I have because I do not want less. No one wants less than more - everybody wants more than less.

Ahhh... yes. More nonsensical claims from these peasants... They state that they are overworked and underpaid, but there's no such thing as overworked or underpaid. You work what you're made to and are paid what you're worth; so, if you're paid little, you're likely worth little!

Despite their complaints of mistreatment, they choose to try and mimic attributes of goodness and generosity - which they cannot possibly possess. What an extreme sign of how pathetic they are. How can one be poor and generous at the same time? They're juxtaposed, right? It is beyond me how some of them, crippled and frail, weak in body and with short life expectancies, can overcome total expiration only with 'high spirits', hope, love and whatever other redundant ideas they claim.

This pathetic category of a social class (or underclass I should say), has always existed since the beginning of civilisation. Their inferiority became noticeable to me during my childhood, when I began to recognize that I was better than the majority; far superior, more intelligent - unsullied. The past is where their rotten roots of poverty lie! We failed to monitor and regulate: the jeopardising increase in population; those undeserving families growing larger in size; peasants living longer than they should; and their children too surpassing their baseline life expectancies - which all led to overcrowding.

Overcrowded streets, slums, shelters, and alleyways. Every space available, occupied by these revolting individuals - diseased, infesting our lives. They even still share shelters with each other in their rookeries; random strangers. Buying and selling from each other with chicken change; two pence, four pence, for absolutely anything, mostly worn-out and second hand. I noticed this was just their woeful attempt at creating their own micro economy – seeing as they cannot survive in the regular economy. They are repugnant!

Because of them, large patches of turf (too close to some of our most highly affluent communities) were turned into flats and tenements for their benefit - and still they complained of a housing shortage. On top of that, they grumble over a lack of jobs. What more do these people want? Just deal with it! Continuously complaining but they never made an attempt to work hard enough to improve their lives. How lazy and sinful.

Every once in a while, we hear of one of the anomalies that worked hard enough to make something of themselves. As for the rest, they're the ones causing the ruin of our country's image, spoiling the appearance of our community's streets and neighbourhoods, causing eyesores in our previously clean neighbourhoods. Is this not also a sin? A sin against our pride, our honour, our dignity? Is it not!? I say it is! They are the living demonstration of sin. Goodness, their mere existence is sinful. So bloody sinful!

Still, at this present day, there is no change. They're still here, multiplying; staining our society, forever sinning. Our great country is still expanding and because of this so-called industrial revolution, all manner of vermin are flocking, herding, and pouring into the cities -

accumulating inside towns, all in search of employment. I mean, the only occupations they're good for and should expect to be allowed into are making, moving, mining, packing and cleaning. Nothing more and everything less.

The worst part of this is that the most hopeless and incompetent of these beings see migration into our greatest cities and towns as their hopeful solution. They chase an optimistic unknown, striving for more than they deserve, in a quest for what they cannot have. Their standard remains poverty and repulsion. They will never be above poverty and repulsion, no matter where they go. This fact will never change! Poverty is their comfort zone, poverty is their success, poverty is their past, poverty is their present, and poverty is their future! Poverty lives in their souls just as prestige lives in mine!

I see us heading towards a future where these individual pieces of dirt - these parasites, still exist as they do now, unless we (the decent and honourable), resolve this seemingly everlasting dichotomy! I see districts and towns full of such revolting beings living in perpetual laziness, lacking the will power to evolve from their animalistic nature! I see potential for improving sewage water, into slightly unclean water with my direction. But let's face it, we're still centuries away from bringing them to a standard anywhere close to fine wine.

I see a possibility of one day transforming the masses into a bearable sight, into a fraction of a fraction of my shadow! I see the road ahead almost completely rid of the lifestyle and attitudes that have cursed their children too - who have infinitely inherited these virtues for generations! Everlastingly poor! Their existence and well-being would be completely irrelevant if they didn't make satisfactory chimney cleaners. This is undeniably their sole purpose for being on earth, and therefore their existence cannot be totally ignored for the pure fact that our chimneys would be exceedingly filthy. They are the hands. A cluster of these humans in our society are still stagnant, no progress, forever poor. No purpose to their lives, living such pointless and futile lives. If money is everything, what does that make someone who has none?

It is a responsibility - no, a providence, to dismiss the worthless beyond repair! For the benefit of all our lives, and most especially theirs. This is the most effective solution for us all to progress forwards."

"...Aaanndd cut! Splendid work, we did that all in one take. Let's take five."

10 - Opportunity

Some things or circumstances only morph into the shape of an opportunity when your perspective merges with your curiosity in a sensational symbiosis. Situations that can be seemingly plain are suddenly intruded by idea and colour. Opportunities exist more often than we see. If our lives are a sum of infinite micro situations that lead us up to every distinct moment, then surely opportunity also occurs on a microscale and therefore, more frequently than we would ordinarily acknowledge.

There are many times when opportunity can present itself more glaringly at the point you are most confused, and the answers are most elusive. This is because your curiosity and urge to know is at a peak and your perspective is most malleable in these situations; we're geared that way. We rarely ever question when things are going right, but always question when they go wrong. Bad or uncomfortable situations have the ability to push us into a curious state of mind and give our point of view enough flexibility to see what we might not have seen before. What was once plain begins to look bright. It is the flawlessly painted picture that we all know as hindsight.

Macro opportunities are life's wildcard - a door or window with potential to change one's experience of life, their knowledge, wisdom, and output. It's the portal to a better alternative. Everything you've been learning and doing gives you the capacity to take advantage of it - but this is granted you have been learning and doing, to recognise when it comes, and take advantage of it. Although it is commonly known to only come around *'once in a lifetime'*, it's certainly not limited to that frequency.

Opportunity can be an unpredictable shapeshifter, with some even morphing into disaster; especially when taken without any consideration. I disagree with the supposed axiom *'take every opportunity'* because some opportunities will be incompatible with the person. Rather, it is more beneficial and rewarding to take an opportunity not just because it appeared, but because it is compatible with the better alternative state you seek for the long term.

If you don't light the match, you can't create a fire, and aside from recognising or searching for opportunity, one can also create it by being proactive. If you seek an alternative circumstance, try the alternative action. You may not have all the variables in your control, but opportunity can be lit, the same way a matchstick can be sparked - the more attempts you make the higher your chances of turning darkness into light. The wonderful thing about trial and error is that it works two-fold. As well as increasing your chances of creating or finding opportunity, you also increase your primary, first-hand experience and learning, on top of wisdom (how to apply all your learnings). You gain the know-how of what to do and what not to do; what triggers, what hinders, what accelerates, what generates, what terminates. In that process, you learn the art of how to be, no matter the context. The key to this idea is proactivity. Nonetheless, many people overstay their time on a so-called "steppingstone" until it inevitably sinks and the opportunity to skip to the next stone disappears - along with their ability or enthusiasm.

You may feel as though it's typically a competitive sport to receive a chance or to catch a break, but sometimes opportunity is just an open door that doesn't necessarily require you to forcefully smash through it - even before someone else. You may have walked into a room you were merely curious about and not even realised the significance. How easy is it to intensely and frantically stress about not having the key for a room, before even checking if the door is already open? In the same way you may have ignored the previous door for that very reason, there's usually someone not far behind, who was either curious enough, found the right perspective, or attempted to spark the match (perhaps even for the umpteenth time) - who simply just wandered through the door without thought of a key. Hopefully, in any case, the core and sole reason you would have dismissed this door was because you knew it wasn't compatible with your person, and not because you didn't have a key…

11 - Another Opportunity

The best form of external opportunity is impacting someone positively in a way which allows them to go and do the same. The critical mass achieved in this cycle is the most invaluable act. It depicts the value of parenthood in a nutshell - the impact a parent has on their child, is the impact their child will have on the world. This type of responsibility is also synonymous with opportunity.

However, in the same manner, various other forms of external opportunity exist, as well as internal opportunity. Will, urge and desire, are examples of internal opportunity. These elements aren't always so easily available or ripe, and certainly not automatically for the right things. It's also not a common reaction for everyone to find the optimal level of willpower to act on a specific task, endeavour or responsibility. Therefore, if you experience this chemistry of ingredients, recognise both the combination and the resulting internal reactions that occur from such, as an opportunity. Partner with it to produce something valuable, fruitful, or exceedingly great. Don't let the spark pass or fizzle out so easily without engaging with it. It may never come back in the same way or even at all. As a result, you will find yourself needing an external jump start in the form of extrinsic motivation - for that once-enthusiastic desire which could have energised your endeavours, but now lies dormant and seemingly lifeless. Consequently, it is pivotal that this zeal (when existent), is earnestly recognised as a significant source of fuel, and genuinely viewed to be an internal opportunity.

12 - Useless Lessons

I have learnt many lessons from many experiences; a lot of which are valuable but not useful to me. Both of which can be true at the same time. Many of these experiences don't actually serve to enhance the future, or only do so in the most minute of ways. It is true that a lot of the lessons 'gained' for the future don't necessarily outweigh the damage or hurt caused in the present, or wounds and scars remembered in the past. They only serve as a relic or picture on the wall of one's life. We try to summon this as inspiration for art of similar proportions and use it to enlighten someone that has less of these experiences themselves - who won't really care much until they have a similar experience of their own. They may also do the same in trying to pass theirs on to someone else. But most of all, this picture's main use is to serve as a tangible souvenir of being a passenger on this unfathomable ride.

13 - Eyes of Assumption

Knowledge of everything is power.
Knowledge of people is everything.
One can never know everything, but one can know people.
People are both the problem and the answer.

I once asked someone, "What major thing have you learnt about people through your life and career?" To which he replied, "They're unpredictable." To this I only partially agree. The reason why we may think like this is because we make assumptions and jump to conclusions (both good and bad), which are either quickly or gradually proven wrong. This reinforces the idea of the nature of unpredictability surrounding people. It has more to do with us and how we think, than them.

Assumptions are necessary to generate new knowledge and to navigate through life more efficiently, because dissecting everything isn't possible. They're heuristics. Mental shortcuts based on patterns we already know, connections we make between the dots that relate; experiences we've had; and ones we know of or heard of (second and third hand). It is perfectly standard and, in many cases, useful to assume. It's the invisible support we rely on to stabilise the infrastructure of our social landscape, and the affair within it.

Assumption determines how we approach or interact with others - how we see others. However, it can sometimes be the very habit to destabilise relationships or trust. The mistake with how assumption is exercised is that more often than not, it takes the form of a flimsy water raft used to cross treacherous, unsettling waters, to reach the uncharted island of uncertain conclusion. When it's wrong, we're disillusioned, and when it's right, we reinforce our bias as truth.

Alternatively, we would do much better to be aware of the type of assumptions we make and why we make them; highlighting them as only assumptions and not a one-way ticket to a certain conclusion. There is a sophistication, tact and balance emanated in constantly evaluating whether an assumption is valid or even necessary, alongside the whys and why nots. Practising this pattern of self-awareness enhances interaction with both people and self, by reducing bias and giving space to objectivity in our relations. Whilst this practice will not provide total immunity from people's display of erraticism, we can become less affected by the discomfort and disappointment of 'unpredictability'.

14 - Communicating in Metaphors

Communication is everything, understanding is more. They both mean more than anything.

Both everything around us and within us is continuously engaging in an infinite exchange of communication and understanding. Our brains with our bodies, nature to itself, God to us, us to each other - a cycle immeasurably interconnected and incalculably critical to life. If communication breaks down, the cycle can't begin. If understanding breaks down, the cycle can't continue. Needless to say, communication supersedes words, and understanding transcends hearing. For life, these two concepts underpin the binary of consciousness. This is understood through the connection a baby shares with its mother or the exchange that can still be had with someone who is deaf or blind.

When it comes to the mind and translating its warehouse of ideas, thoughts, or memories (to the level just beneath tangible), language is key. Your perception can never be regarded if you aren't able to articulate yourself in a way that can be understood by at least one person - other than yourself. Someone else or something else must be on the reciprocating end, who can receive and interpret your intention. You can have the greatest idea ever, but you must sharpen the skill of communicating it to someone other than yourself. Understanding on the receiving end is what makes the formula work, especially in the context of a relationship. It should be sought after by either party. That being said, the style of communication can contribute to aiding understanding on the receiving end - meaning the communicator ought to understand how they can best communicate. There is also a time or moment that something can be said, to fall on more attuned ears and be better understood.

In a perfect world these two things (communication and understanding) meet in the middle. In a non-perfect world, it is vital for at least one to be emphasised well. It goes without saying that two bad communicators engaging is a recipe for disappointment (it helps if the other person is good or composed). I would choose to emphasise understanding, because by proxy it also provides what can be referred to as 'overstanding' (a view of the entire scope). It submits to what it means to be human - trying to piece together information to make crystal clear sense of it and thus, life. Although particles of meaning are bound to fall through the cracks sometimes, understanding works overtime to hoover them out. If you can't capture the details, capture the sentiment; if you can't capture the sentiment, capture the details. If you can, capture both the sentiment and the details - eventually the meaning will surface.

On the other hand, if you choose to emphasise communication, a tool that can be utilised, is one I term **'just enough articulation'**

(JEA). It acts as a rope for the other person to grab onto in an attempt to understand what was intended, and is a process that can prompt or position the communicator for additional samples of articulation until enough understanding is reached. A good example of JEA is the use of similes.

A lie is like a microbe that contaminates all forms of communication, and just like a microbe, it multiplies in excess until it's confident or safe enough to continue asserting itself. The catch 22 is that somehow, telling the truth all the time apparently (according to social sources), isn't ideal either - and oddly enough is received as very strange behaviour when practically carried out.

From when you're born, the world lies to you, and so you get used to being surrounded by lies. Some are bigger than others and not everyone even realises when they believe one or are telling one - even to themselves. It becomes an innate predisposition and one who has not purposely strived to purge this practice may even eventually lie to themselves. None of this actually looks or seems out of place because many societal infrastructures are founded on lies. Parents, family, friends, culture, media, marketing, government. Circumstances remain like this because such structures stand too tall and too important to be compromised and shattered. Each steel beam and window, too integral to the design of the world - and the truth, regardless of the angle it travels from, would be the stone thrown either within or at the glass house.

Conversely, it won't be thrown at all or if thrown it won't reach, for reasons that will be determined by context. But it can still be categorised as an immune system response or the guarding of the gatekeepers. Either way, the current conditions will stay this way for a while, because it costs a great amount to tell the truth. The truth is, much of this infrastructure was built with debt, and the only way to sustain it all, is to incur more debt. One day this debt will become ever so expensive - if that isn't the case already.

The greatest and most impactful communicator isn't necessarily someone who can deliver a speech, but someone who can tell a pure uncontaminated truth and make it understandable. Telling the truth is a striking art, and you are likely to be misunderstood - just like art can be misunderstood. Even the power and profoundness of art is determined by the amount of truth it conveys. Art is a direct distillation of meaning.

Bearers of pure truth are few and far between, in the same way that absolute truth is - and only a few things represent such (when compared to what doesn't). These truth bearers end-up being marginalised, made to be delusional, or killed by society and its gatekeepers for threatening its infrastructure. This is the present-day version of a stoning ceremony - prepared against a real asset, rather than the glass house. Some food for thought about who some of these individuals could be through history...

Communication is a toolbox for conveying or extracting meaning, and language is merely a tool - a vastly potent one. The biblical story of the Tower of Babel is the first evidence of the exceeding power of language; if wielded correctly, and the limitless potential of understanding. God himself validates this through his values, as well as in that story.

It is perfectly possible to use the same tool for many purposes. It is also possible to use the right tool for the wrong purpose, and continuously so. The outcome is frankly, poor results and the tiresome weight of frustration. Although we can initially somewhat communicate when we're born, we start off terrible at doing so. We don't have many tools in our communication toolbox except crying or crying. We are quite under equipped to extract much out of people and life - let alone comprehend. Unless you've already had years of tool selection practice through plenty of interactions and contexts (nurture), or had been simply gifted (nature), you would need to be deliberate about cultivating this skill.

Aside from Grice's Maxims, four other pillars uphold conversational success. Of these four pillars, two involve evaluation and the other two, action. Each one is seemingly simple, but in the complex labyrinth of language and conversational communication, simplicity is an ideal starting point. Most people may exercise a lot of these organically, however, intentional awareness of them influences a conversation's effectiveness.

1. **Listen.** This is a tool which will assist you in extracting the most out of an exchange - I like to think of it as observation with your ears. It's not just about getting out what you want

to say. To be able to execute listening effectively you must suppress any reactive, involuntary response - unless in acknowledgement of what is being said. Fully put yourself in the other's shoes and experience what they are saying. Purely listening and fighting the urge to prepare your next words while the other party is speaking, will allow you to select the best tool for the situation and lead you to the most appropriate next words. Getting this correct, provides a better chance of uttering something more meaningful. One major reason why we can be inclined to converse with prepared responses in our back pocket is because we are uncomfortable with moments of 'awkwardness' or silence. But acknowledging and going over more ambiguous parts of what was said by the other person helps to avoid this, as well as reinforces your understanding.

2. **Read the room & reciprocate.** It's vital to recognise the context of the conversation and other actors such as the mood, tone and intention of the other person. Having a sense of self-awareness alongside paying attention to these factors, sharpens your instinct to reciprocate appropriately; and appropriate reciprocation upholds a mutual respect for the conversation.

3. **Ask a question.** Questions promote room for even more listening - as listening is the principal and most versatile tool at our disposal. It can be used in most situations and even addresses the issue of awkward silences in a more productive

manner. Creating or finding an opportunity to listen should be the goal; questions are the instrument.

4. **Summarise.** Communication serves to convey and extract meaning; the outcome of a conversation must capture this essence. A summary is a neat way to wrap a conversational exchange and can include reinforcing the purpose; making clear what was gained; highlighting the understanding that you picked up; or simply stating your position or actions following the discussion. Readdressing one of the main statements that you picked up whilst listening, goes some way in concluding a conversation wholesomely.

15 - Misunderstood

If you sometimes feel misunderstood, you could perhaps just be onto something that no one else yet sees. On the other hand, if you always feel completely understood the first-time round, then are you being honest in all those instances? Are you compromising any amount of authenticity? Saying what you think out loud can often be misinterpreted at first instance. Even so, don't simplify yourself, or your thinking for anyone else - except to explain.

There's no shame in being misunderstood. As frustrating as it is, it's inevitable. Firstly, it is actually people's right of choice whether they want to try and understand you or not - and they won't always give you that opportunity. Whether they have the perspective or capacity to, is a separate matter. An extensive list of great people who were misunderstood in some form or another would stretch for pages. Although, on this occasion, without exhausting that list, we can identify a few of these case studies that can be learnt from.

Nicolaus Copernicus and his now axiomatic heliocentric theory - later supported by Galileo. Ludwig van Beethoven and his igneous compositions. Vincent Van Gogh and his inspirational impasto paintings. Leonardo da Vinci and his revolutionary creations and concepts. Nikola Tesla and innovative AC technology. Martin Luther

King and his peaceful dream. Malcolm X and his assertive vision. Rosa Parks and her ground-breaking protest. Virgin Mary and her divine baby birth. Jesus Christ and his transcendent teachings.

The underpinning point is that great characters and their great ideas are greatly misconstrued or mistook. Some are never understood. And some only are after they die; decades and centuries after their ideas or opinions were born. However, the originality, significance and potency of their message is never diluted, even over time.

Maybe don't take it to heart when misunderstood. The greatest artwork is often misunderstood. Such art is painted by characters who tell the truth. In reference to *'Communicating in Metaphors'*, all that is ever really necessary, is to convince just one other person to understand your point of view, if you believe it's worth knowing.

It is true that you can never reach full, absolute comprehension of anything or anyone that is really worth the curious pursuit. It's a gradual and bottomless journey of discovery, with occasional spikes of significant eureka moments. These findings continue to ignite a constant curiosity and desire to know, uncover and peel back infinite layers.

Illusion is ever perpetual. Every time you think you've sussed the answer, more questions are raised, and more alternatives appear. It is for this same reason why many would retire from their quest for answers. However, it is also the same reason we must continue searching for them, and not be satisfied with incomprehension, confusion or missed understanding. Every day is an opportunity to understand something or someone. In that process, there will be moments at which you misunderstand, but the more you ruminate and adjust your angle the more likely you are to reach a eureka moment.

Pause to ponder…

16 - The Best Chapter Ever

Your notion here…

17 - Self-actualization

Fulfilment is fundamental. People typically speak of doing what makes you 'happy', but this is a dangerous and short-sighted way of thinking. Happiness can dissipate just as quickly as seconds on a clock. Any emotion can change with the wind, just as easily as they were inspired.

However, fulfilment is a foundation that can't be unsettled just as easily once established. It is a more enduring state. There is a sense of contentment that both happiness and fulfilment provide, which is the reason they are continually misinterpreted as the same thing. Fulfilment is the real satisfaction people subconsciously seek whenever they say they're 'looking for happiness' - they just aren't directly aware of it or how to go about finding it. It is instead much easier to fill that expensive void with a cheap alternative.

Our larger purpose on earth cannot solely be to find boosts of happiness, but rather to live out a full and filled life. Different sources of happiness present much inconsistency, diminishing returns, or will likely come with an expiry date attached - if not, could actually signify a source of fulfilment. Eating your favourite food on any one given day will make you happy. Eating it every day for the rest of your life, will not contribute to multiplying or compounding this short-lived happiness. It will rather give birth to a baby void that grows as it's over fed an obsessive, excessive, unhealthy diet. This is the kind of behaviour which drives you into deficit and can even evoke the opposite of happiness.

If you seek happiness itself, it will continuously elude you till you have to seek it again. If you seek fulfilment, you will transcend happiness. Contrary to what is preached, don't build your life around things that make you happy, but rather what makes you fulfilled. You will know what your personal source of fulfilment is because it is what will consistently satisfy your being, even when it doesn't necessarily make you happy.

Finding or achieving the said thing is no easy feat for many, so don't be disheartened or confused if you haven't yet. Not many people even reach the stage of epiphany. Some are instinctively more sensitive or attuned to what their self-fulfilment looks like, and others must intentionally pursue this. It is not essential from the beginning, to have full knowledge of what brings you true, unending contentment; but it is essential to have awareness of its overall importance, as it is the ingredient which inspires meaning and jolts life into your work, labour, and efforts. This oasis of fulfilment is like the pot of gold at the end of the rainbow, a place which can be found at the intersection where discipline meets freedom.

What we need primarily in order to self-actualize, is time - of which we've been given an appropriate amount. Time to think, or do, or at the very least try - even if that is achieved by process of elimination and trial and error. Focus on finding the environment or activity that really tickles an endless curiosity within you; or one which feels effortless, natural, or tolerable to you, despite others typically finding it difficult, inconvenient, or impossible. Once you establish these coordinates you can begin to dig as deep as ever - you have discovered the location of your hidden treasure.

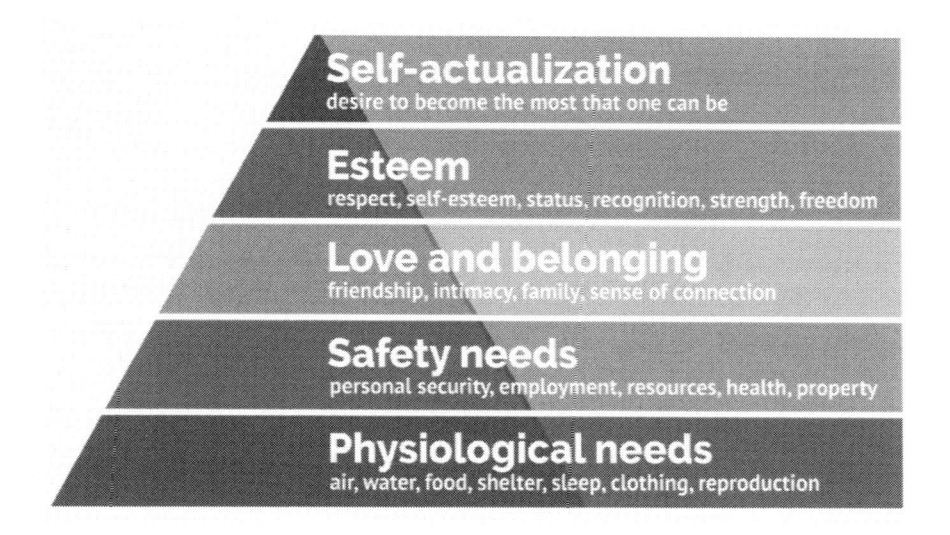

Self-actualization
desire to become the most that one can be

Esteem
respect, self-esteem, status, recognition, strength, freedom

Love and belonging
friendship, intimacy, family, sense of connection

Safety needs
personal security, employment, resources, health, property

Physiological needs
air, water, food, shelter, sleep, clothing, reproduction

Self-actualization is the peak we innately desire to reach in Maslow's hierarchy of needs. However, the other stages of the pyramid form the fundamental components needed to reach this self-fulfilment. This framework is not constrained by time, and you can self-actualise at any point. Climbing and reaching the peak of this pyramid is the ultimate attainment and fulfilment. Abiding at the top is another dimension of experience entirely.

Even though there are no set methods, routes, or time frames for scaling this pyramid (except the ones personally set), climbing systematically from the bottom up is the obvious and conventional route, and one that makes the most chronological sense. All the main elements underlined, from physiological needs, safety needs, love and belonging, and esteem, should typically take place in linear order (given civil and social constructs, as well as our understanding of them). Maslow even argued that deprivation of the needs at various stages of the pyramid may lead to illness in an individual, either mental or physical.

Most usually postpone the full pursuit of self-actualization till the later stage of their life. After all, your life experiences and perhaps well-constructed stability by that point, should make you more equipped to understand yourself, and invest the rest of your days into exploring other areas of life's simulation. You've perhaps done what you 'needed' to do at the start of your life and now have the urge to take on what you 'wanted' to do for the rest; but this is a gamble. You only 'hope' to one day have 'enough' time or freedom or money, to then go after self-actualization.

But what if you can't? What if life does its thing and takes more turns than the ones you had accounted for? Worse yet, what if you get to your envisioned checkpoint and realise, you're in fact actually lost, tired and weary from all the prior work or wear and tear? Your mind lacks inspiration, your being lacks soul, your soul lacks fire, and your body lacks vim. You don't have to tick every box within every phase of the pyramid to move upwards. It is far more crucial that you self-actualise, than when. Inevitably, those that do, will do so at different times.

Lack of self-actualization is an epidemic. Only a few are actually fortunate enough (or determined enough) to reach self-actualization, and a fraction of that few do so without overly respecting each stage conventionally or at all. What you can control is how much time and effort you allocate to each phase and what methods you use to navigate through them. It's up to the individual to decide. One doesn't have to put it off till way down the line, when they've done every other thing under the sun. A linear route doesn't necessarily mean a long route, and as Maslow highlighted, you can later return to a deficient need that was previously skipped or lost. There is always an option to take a more arbitrary approach.

Have a plan. It's ok to amend it and play as you go. The plan doesn't have to be a detailed account of war and peace, or become legislative law, but even an outline serves decisively well. How else will you know when you've deviated from truth, light, goals, aspirations, or anything good for that matter? How else will you know where you are, or even how lost you are? Of course, with a vague map you can still be momentarily lost, but without any map you're borderline hopeless and at the mercy of pure fortune. The thick fog obstructing your vision of the top will begin to dissipate once you do have a plan and start to enact it. You'll also feel less confused and aimless, which is pivotal to progressing - because confusion is an intangible kryptonite that is the number one adversary of progress.

18 - Super Set

There is a philosophical way about the mechanics of exercising which makes it an intriguing and beneficial construct to dissect. Countless existential truths and gems are embedded in our interaction with voluntary, self-imposed physical strain. We know about the many benefits attached to training the body and are also well aware of the severe inconveniences that precede those benefits. Whether one sees it as torture or discipline is purely subjective.

You don't necessarily need an intellectual ruler to be able to draw the philosophical parallels between exercise and life. Yes, the comparisons are indeed subtle, but in fact clear, and it is evident in those intricacies and interconnections, that the rudimentary learnings gained from physical training, are extractions also fundamental to life.

Growth - Growing, in any capacity, is the primary consequence of exercise and the fundamental essence of life. In the gym you must work to tear your muscle fibres before they can be rebuilt bigger and stronger, and sometimes the same procedure must take place in life. This is primarily how growth occurs.

Playing the cards you're dealt with - Genetically we're not all born the same, and comparatively will need to work harder in different areas than others. Likewise, we will also have genetic advantages and uniqueness over others in some areas. We have different predispositions, physiological responses, and capacities. Our fitness experiences or journeys may start at different points and be accelerated at different rates, but we can all establish a personal optimum and manoeuvre towards that. It is not conducive to chase after someone else's optimum; people will do identical things and obtain different results. Similarly, life doesn't hand everyone the same starting point, but that doesn't mean an automatic loss lies ahead. Organise the cards you do have at your disposal and play them as best as you can.

Consistency - The more regularly you do it, the better you get at it and the more control you gain over the output. This is the same no matter the physical activity and a repeatable formula across the different facets of life.

Patience - This is the act of waiting with expectation as well as perspective. Patience is the intersection where both ambition and humility coexist. Your immediate inputs don't instantly materialise as results. It is unrealistic to expect visible results from doing a week's worth of exercise in a day. No matter how enormous that one-given effort is, it is intentionally designed that we have to wait out a repeated gradual effort, or an incubation period, to earn our rewards.

Ambition - Ambition doesn't look the same amongst people, but it sounds the same - you can always hear its tone. To achieve any type of success (whether self-defined or universal) you must liaise with ambition. Your level of ambition naturally becomes your personal measurement for success. It is how you can gauge if you've achieved your own version of success or are at least on the path to doing so.

Strength & Conditioning - Strength is developed from undertaking a bigger burden than you're comfortable carrying - but just about able to. Conditioning comes from subjecting yourself to difficult conditions, which you become more built to withstand. Even if the challenge doesn't become easier you become more equipped to resist or endure it. The amount you can bear is usually more than you actually think you can.

Pushing past limits / Failure - Expanding beyond barriers is paramount to achieving any momentous results. Overload is the key component for strength as it is for breaking boundaries. Greatness comes not from pushing to the limit but past the limit and failing your way to success. The representation of this in gym terms is lifting till 'failure'. A failure rep is the rep you attempt after the final one which you barely completed; sometimes you might need the help of a spot (meaning assistance in gym-speak) to do so. Through this, you learn why failure is not only necessary but inevitable before achievement, and why help may be critical to reaching your goal along the way. It is an asset to master the mind because your relationship with limits and failures will be enhanced for the better.

Leaving your comfort zone - The only thing threatened by the pursuit of achievement is your comfort zone. Said comfort zone is already a territory that belongs to you, however every time you quest and venture out of it, is an opportunity to conquer new ground and expand that zone even further - giving you more freedom in new areas of life. The present inhabitants of that potentially additional territory will differ for every individual, from fear to ignorance, laziness, or a combination of multiple other antagonists. They will pose a self-induced challenge to take on, outside of what you're used to; but the harder option is usually the most rewarding.

Lifestyle - Exercise is a very self-centred activity. It is about the individual achieving aspirations, confronting themselves and tackling challenges. This focus on self should be taken seriously, as it creates an outlet for expression in a way that is more crucial to survival or thriving than we may realise. It is a practice that can be mastered just like any other skill - by being sewn and interwoven into our lifestyle. Our engagement with physical training reinforces our ability to cultivate more intrinsic motivation, and rely less on extrinsic incentives - if done healthily. This is a vital and reliable power source not only for training and working out, but even more so for other significant segments of life.

Form - By prioritising good form, you can achieve greater exercise results while minimising the risk of injury. A solid form ensures that you execute movements correctly and build the habit of precision - this is vital for promoting efficient and effective training. Cultivating a sturdy posture in life is imperative. In this way, great form can be likened to great organisation, coordination, and structure in your daily living. It serves as a framework of support in all contexts, by reinforcing positive muscle memory to enhance how you navigate or manoeuvre through life. Fine form promotes sustainable success - longevity is the aim and form is the linchpin.

Injury - Getting injured happens. It hurts. Sometimes you recover quickly, sometimes you don't. How will it affect your journey moving forward?

Rest - The importance of rest is non-negotiable. It is essential for repair and recovery, as well as making sure all the benefits that you gain through exercise are well embedded and even enjoyed. It is intriguing and humbling how imperative recuperation is to our makeup and function. Nothing can exist as it does without it. This applies to our efforts and pursuits, as well as the advantages and gains we derive from it. Even God rested.

19 - Stream of Consciousness

Can every idea be articulated?

Do birds suffer from depression?

What makes people look like their name?

Does a good artist always recognise the depth of their own creativity?

What are analogies, and why do they make so much sense?

Is it ok to inspire through false representation?

Is it ok to give sound advice that you wouldn't even follow?

What would be the most appropriate favourite and least favourite thing in life?

Which bible characters did or did not make heaven and why? Would we be shocked?

Is there an optimal level of freedom or discipline and can there be diminishing returns (to this)?

Life. Who actually writes this stuff? It's unbelievable.

Are we still now, who we used to be before?

What is the most optimal time to wake up?

What is the best time to sleep?

Who is the most known person to ever live?

Top 5 greatest human heroes ever?

Person from history who couldn't survive the 21st century and why?

Person from history who will excel the most in the 21st century and why?

What should be the most universally agreed fear?

If you got to do it again, what would you do differently?

How different would life be if time and dates were measured differently?

Are we in charge of our own destiny, or is fate?

How did cliché even become cliché?

What is a thought?

How are the thoughts in our physical brain separate from our mind and soul?

Should everybody be given a second chance? If not, where should the line be drawn?

What is love?

What is hate?

Why is emotion so potent yet intangible?

If you 'feel' love but don't act on it, does it count? And if you don't 'feel' any love but act in a way that shows it, does it count?

How objective can art be?

Do we actually need bad for good to be good? Why can't we just have good?

In a mutual bond between two people, can they both feel the exact same way?

What happens chemically and spiritually during heartbreak?

What is the number one reason why relationships with people are so necessary in life?

Is any human capable of uncorrupted power?

Why do so many people not care about their purpose or life's meaning?

Is philosophy pointless?

Why do evil people do so well and get away with so much?

What are fruits and why are they actually tasty?

How was the first language even created? How does one go about creating a language from scratch?

Does language influence thoughts, or are they mutually exclusive?

Could we think the same things without language, and what would that look like?

What is the most ignored or dismissed truth?

What is the most believed or adopted lie?

Does equality exist, or is it an illusion?

How many other earths are there in the universe, and are things elsewhere playing out the same or differently?

How many versions of humanity have there been before us that were possibly wiped off the face of earth, or advanced so far that they left?

If there can never be two of the same people, what is the closest version to yourself another human has been without being you? What were they missing in order to fully become you?

How bad could the state of affairs get on earth?

What era would be the best to live in?

What are animals even thinking?

How sophisticated are animal languages?

Do animals and insects have souls?

How come wise people hardly have many friends?

Is there one actual secret ingredient to success that no one has yet put their finger on - including successful people?

Is life flashing before your eyes real?

Is there one type of thought or feeling that only people who die have, right before they die, or on the day they die - but is exclusive to these individuals only?

What was the best thing before sliced bread?

What is the best thing since sliced bread?

What is the optimal measure for success?

What is humour?

What is the most efficient way to crack a numeric passcode or password?

What is a memory? How is a memory formed, captured, and stored?

Can a memory be captured and stored outside of the brain and inputted into the brain?

What happens to a lost memory, and can it ever be retrieved?

When you lose a train of thought, is it gone forever, or does it resurface down the line as a new thought that you didn't actually realise you had before?

Is any memory actually really lost in the brain or is it just irretrievable?

What is déjà vu?

What are coincidences?

What makes up me?

How many people are thinking or saying the exact same thing as me at the exact same time?

Why do we dream?

Has anyone ever had the same exact dream as me?

Do animals dream?

Do they also have ambition?

How many thoughts do we have in a lifetime?

How many grains of rice, strands of spaghetti or noodles, pieces of chicken, or slices of bread have we eaten in our life?

Will all the innovative technology we create from now, only be a continuous variation or enhancement of what we already have, or will we ever invent anything cosmically radical again - like the phone or computer? And how long until we do?

Is it better to be a night person or a morning person?

Is it possible to never lie once through life, and what would that look like?

How often did civilians travel or take holidays before planes?

How were borders of different regions and countries patrolled before passports?

Will it one day be possible to project a human brain onto a screen in the form of an understandable illustration?

Is there life after death?

Is God real?

Are we all the offspring of the first created man?

How many humans have ever lived?

Have any superhumans ever existed?

How much have the pictures and accounts of history been manipulated, and who would be responsible?

How many facts are lost or missing, and how much is fabricated?

Have we been deprived of any crucial information in history, which would have accelerated the advancement of civilization past the point we are now?

How true is the bible? Have any parts been manipulated through time?

Did Jesus really exist as the human son of a divine God?

Why do all religious writings and practices claim to be the truth?

Has someone been fooling with us all?

How and when can we find out the whole truth?

Would we be able to handle the whole truth, and would it transform how we're currently living?

What is truth?

20 - Collage of God

- "In the beginning God created the heavens and the earth…" - Genesis

- "So God created mankind in his own image, in the image of God he created them; male and female he created them…" - Genesis

- "And God saw everything that he had made, and, behold, it was very good…"- Genesis

- "'Do not come any closer,' God said. 'Take off your sandals, for the place where you are standing is holy ground.' Then he said, 'I am the God of your father, the God of Abraham, the God of Isaac and the God of Jacob.' At this, Moses hid his face, because he was afraid to look at God." - Exodus

- "And God said, 'I will be with you. And this will be the sign to you that it is I who have sent you: When you have brought the people out of Egypt, you will worship God on this mountain.' Moses said to God, 'Suppose I go to the Israelites and say to them, The God of your fathers has sent me to you, and they ask me, What is his name? Then what shall I tell them?' God said to Moses, 'I am who I am. This is what you are to say to the Israelites: I am has sent me to you.' God also said to Moses, 'Say to the Israelites, The Lord, the God of your fathers—the God of Abraham, the God of Isaac and the God of Jacob—has sent me to you. This is my name forever, the name you shall call me from generation to generation.'" - Exodus

- "'But,' he said, 'you cannot see my face, for no one may see me and live.'" - Exodus

- "I am the Lord, who brought you up out of Egypt to be your God; therefore be holy, because I am holy." - Leviticus

- "God is not human, that he should lie, not a human being, that he should change his mind. Does he speak and then not act? Does he promise and not fulfil?" - Numbers

- "For the Lord your God is a consuming fire, a jealous God." - Deuteronomy

- "He is the Rock, his works are perfect, and all his ways are just. A faithful God who does no wrong, upright and just is he." - Deuteronomy

- "For the Lord your God dried up the Jordan before you until you had crossed over. The Lord your God did to the Jordan what he had done to the Red Sea when he dried it up before us until we had crossed over. He did this so that all the peoples of the earth might know that the hand of the Lord is powerful and so that you might always fear the Lord your God." - Joshua

- "You know with all your heart and soul that not one of all the good promises the Lord your God gave you has failed. Every promise has been fulfilled; not one has failed." - Joshua

- "Now fear the Lord and serve him with all faithfulness. Throw away the gods your ancestors worshipped beyond the Euphrates River and in Egypt, and serve the Lord." - Joshua

- "I said to you, I am the Lord your God; do not worship the gods of the Amorites, in whose land you live. But you have not listened to me." - Judges

- "I went away full, but the Lord has brought me back empty. Why call me Naomi? The Lord has afflicted me; the Almighty has brought misfortune upon me." - Ruth

- "May the Lord repay you for what you have done. May you be richly rewarded by the Lord, the God of Israel, under whose wings you have come to take refuge." - Ruth

- "There is no one holy like the Lord; there is no one besides you; there is no Rock like our God." - 1 Samuel

- "Do not keep talking so proudly or let your mouth speak such arrogance, for the Lord is a God who knows, and by him deeds are weighed. The Lord brings death and makes alive; he brings down to the grave and raises up." - 1 Samuel

- "As for God, his way is perfect: The Lord's word is flawless; he shields all who take refuge in him. For who is God besides the Lord? And who is the Rock except our God? It is God who arms me with strength and keeps my way secure." - 2 Samuel

- "Lord, the God of Israel, there is no God like you in heaven above or on earth below—you who keep your covenant of love with your servants who continue wholeheartedly in your way." - 1 Kings

- "And Hezekiah prayed to the Lord: 'Lord, the God of Israel, enthroned between the cherubim, you alone are God over all the kingdoms of the earth. You have made heaven and earth.'" - 2 Kings

- "David praised the Lord in the presence of the whole assembly, saying, 'Praise be to you, Lord, the God of our father Israel, from everlasting to everlasting. Yours, Lord, is the greatness and the power and the glory and the majesty and the splendour, for everything in heaven and earth is yours. Yours, Lord, is the kingdom; you are exalted as head over all. Wealth and honour come from you; you are the ruler of all things. In your hands are strength and power to exalt and give strength to all.'" - 1 Chronicles

- "Lord, the God of our ancestors, are you not the God who is in heaven? You rule over all the kingdoms of the nations. Power and might are in your hand, and no one can withstand you." - 2 Chronicles

- "Lord, the God of Israel, you are righteous! We are left this day as a remnant. Here we are before you in our guilt, though because of it not one of us can stand in your presence." - Ezra

- "Lord, the God of heaven, the great and awesome God, who keeps his covenant of love with those who love him and keep his commandments," - Nehemiah

- "Indeed, I know that this is true. But how can mere mortals prove their innocence before God? Though they wished to dispute with him, they could not answer him one time out of a thousand. His wisdom is profound, his power is vast. Who has resisted him and come out unscathed? He moves mountains without their knowing it and overturns them in his anger. He shakes the earth from its place and makes its pillars tremble. He speaks to the sun and it does not shine; he seals off the light of the stars. He alone stretches out the heavens and treads on the waves of the sea. He is the Maker of the Bear and Orion, the Pleiades and the constellations of the south. He performs wonders that cannot be fathomed, miracles that cannot be counted. When he passes me, I cannot see him; when he goes by, I cannot perceive him. If he snatches away, who can stop him? Who can say to him, 'What are you doing?' God does not restrain his anger; even the cohorts of Rahab cowered at his feet. How then can I dispute with him? How can I find words to argue with him? Though I were innocent, I could not answer him; I could only plead with my Judge for mercy. Even if I summoned him and he responded, I do not believe he would give me a hearing. He would crush me with a storm and multiply my wounds for no reason. He would not let me catch my breath but would overwhelm me with misery. If it is a matter of strength, he is mighty! And if it is a matter of justice, who can challenge him? Even if I were innocent, my mouth would condemn me; if I were blameless, it would pronounce me guilty. Although I am blameless, I have no concern for myself; I despise my own life. It is all the same; that is why I say, 'He destroys both the blameless and the wicked.' When a scourge brings sudden death, he mocks the despair of the innocent. When a land falls into the hands of the wicked, he blindfolds its judges. If it is not he, then who is it? My days are swifter than a runner; they fly away without a glimpse of joy. They skim past like boats of papyrus, like eagles swooping down on their prey. If I say, 'I will forget my complaint, I will change my expression, and smile,' I still dread all my sufferings, for I know you will not hold me innocent. Since I am already found guilty, why should I struggle in vain? Even if I washed myself with soap and my hands with cleansing powder, you would plunge me into a slime pit so that even my clothes would detest me. He is not a mere mortal like me that I might answer him, that we might confront each other in court. If only there were someone to mediate between us, someone to bring us together, someone to remove God's rod from me, so that his terror would frighten me no more. Then I would speak up without fear of him, but as it now stands with me, I cannot." - Job

- "The heavens declare the glory of God; the skies proclaim the work of his hands. Day after day they pour forth speech; night after night they reveal knowledge. They have no speech, they use no words; no sound is heard from them. Yet their voice goes out into all the earth, their words to the ends of the world. In the heavens God has pitched a tent for the sun." - Psalms

- "He says, 'Be still, and know that I am God; I will be exalted among the nations, I will be exalted in the earth.'" - Psalms

- "The fear of the Lord is the beginning of knowledge, but fools despise wisdom and instruction." - Proverbs

- "The fear of the Lord is the beginning of wisdom, and knowledge of the Holy One is understanding." - Proverbs

- "What do workers gain from their toil? I have seen the burden God has laid on the human race. He has made everything beautiful in its time. He has also set eternity in the human heart; yet no one can fathom what God has done from beginning to end. I know that everything God does will endure forever; nothing can be added to it and nothing taken from it. God does it so that people will fear him." - Ecclesiastes

- "Do you not know? Have you not heard? The Lord is the everlasting God, the Creator of the ends of the earth. He will not grow tired or weary, and his understanding no one can fathom."- Isaiah

- "Ah, Sovereign Lord, you have made the heavens and the earth by your great power and outstretched arm. Nothing is too hard for you. You show love to thousands but bring the punishment for the parents' sins into the laps of their children after them. Great and mighty God, whose name is the Lord Almighty, great are your purposes and mighty are your deeds. Your eyes are open to the ways of all mankind; you reward each person according to their conduct and as their deeds deserve." - Jeremiah

- "Because of the Lord's great love we are not consumed, for his compassions never fail. They are new every morning; great is your faithfulness." - Lamentations

- "I saw that from what appeared to be his waist up he looked like glowing metal, as if full of fire, and that from there down he looked like fire; and brilliant light surrounded him. Like the appearance of a rainbow in the clouds on a rainy day, so was the radiance around him. This was the appearance of the likeness of the glory of the Lord. When I saw it, I fell facedown, and I heard the voice of one speaking." - Ezekiel

- "I am the Lord your God; follow my decrees and be careful to keep my laws." - Ezekiel

- "For he is the living God and he endures forever; his kingdom will not be destroyed, his dominion will never end. He rescues and he saves; he performs signs and wonders in the heavens and on the earth. He has rescued Daniel from the power of the lions." - Daniel

- "As I looked, thrones were set in place, and the Ancient of Days took his seat. His clothing was as white as snow; the hair of his head was white like wool. His throne was flaming with fire, and its wheels were all ablaze. A river of fire was flowing, coming out from before him. Thousands upon thousands attended him; ten thousand times ten thousand stood before him. The court was seated, and the books were opened." - Daniel

- "But I have been the Lord your God ever since you came out of Egypt. You shall acknowledge no God but me, no Saviour except me." - Hosea

- "Rend your heart and not your garments. Return to the Lord your God, for he is gracious and compassionate, slow to anger and abounding in love, and he relents from sending calamity." - Joel

- "He who made the Pleiades and Orion, who turns midnight into dawn and darkens day into night, who calls for the waters of the sea and pours them out over the face of the land— the Lord is his name." - Amos

- "The day of the Lord is near for all nations. As you have done, it will be done to you; your deeds will return upon your own head." - Obadiah

- "I knew that you are a gracious and compassionate God, slow to anger and abounding in love, a God who relents from sending calamity." - Jonah

- "Look! The Lord is coming from his dwelling place; he comes down and treads on the heights of the earth. The mountains melt beneath him and the valleys split apart, like wax before the fire, like water rushing down a slope." - Micah

- "Who is a God like you, who pardons sin and forgives the transgression of the remnant of his inheritance? You do not stay angry forever but delight to show mercy." - Micah

- "The Lord is a jealous and avenging God; the Lord takes vengeance and is filled with wrath. The Lord takes vengeance on his foes and vents his wrath against his enemies. The Lord is slow to anger but great in power; the Lord will not leave the guilty unpunished. His way is in the whirlwind and the storm, and clouds are the dust of his feet. He rebukes the sea and dries it up; he makes all the rivers run dry. Bashan and Carmel wither and the blossoms of Lebanon fade. The mountains quake before him and the hills melt away. The earth trembles at his presence, the world and all who live in it. Who can withstand his indignation? Who can endure his fierce anger? His wrath is poured out like fire; the rocks are shattered before him. The Lord is good, a refuge in times of trouble. He cares for those who trust in him." - Nahum

- "God came from Teman, the Holy One from Mount Paran. His glory covered the heavens and his praise filled the earth. His splendour was like the sunrise; rays flashed from his hand, where his power was hidden. Plague went before him; pestilence followed his steps. He stood, and shook the earth; he looked, and made the nations tremble. The ancient mountains crumbled and the age-old hills collapsed— but he marches on forever." - Habakkuk

- "Be silent before the Sovereign Lord, for the day of the Lord is near." - Zephaniah

- "This is what the Lord Almighty says: 'In a little while I will once more shake the heavens and the earth, the sea and the dry land. I will shake all nations, and what is desired by all nations will come, and I will fill this house with glory,' says the Lord Almighty. 'The silver is mine and the gold is mine,' declares the Lord Almighty. 'The glory of this present house will be greater than the glory of the former house,' says the Lord Almighty. 'And in this place I will grant peace,' declares the Lord Almighty." - Haggai

- "The Lord will be king over the whole earth. On that day there will be one Lord, and his name the only name." -

Zechariah

- "'For I am a great king,' says the Lord Almighty, 'and my name is to be feared among the nations.'" - Malachi

- "God is the biggest name. The order amidst chaos, the peace amidst fear, the light amidst darkness, the right amidst wrong, the composition amidst void, the solution amidst problem, the question and the answer, the owner and master of time; invincible, invisible, yet perceivable." – Hans

21 - Son of Man

- "When the Son of Man comes in his glory, and all the angels with him, he will sit on his glorious throne. All the nations will be gathered before him, and he will separate the people one from another as a shepherd separates the sheep from the goats. He will put the sheep on his right and the goats on his left. Then the King will say to those on his right, 'Come, you who are blessed by my Father; take your inheritance, the kingdom prepared for you since the creation of the world. For I was hungry and you gave me something to eat, I was thirsty and you gave me something to drink, I was a stranger and you invited me in, I needed clothes and you clothed me, I was sick and you looked after me, I was in prison and you came to visit me.' Then the righteous will answer him, 'Lord, when did we see you hungry and feed you, or thirsty and give you something to drink? When did we see you a stranger and invite you in, or needing clothes and clothe you? When did we see you sick or in prison and go to visit you?' The King will reply, 'Truly I tell you, whatever you did for one of the least of these brothers and sisters of mine, you did for me.' Then he will say to those on his left, 'Depart from me, you who are cursed, into the eternal fire prepared for the devil and his angels. For I was hungry and you gave me nothing to eat, I was thirsty and you gave me nothing to drink, I was a stranger and you did not invite me in, I needed clothes and you did not clothe me, I was sick and in prison and you did not look after me.' They also will answer, 'Lord, when did we see you hungry or thirsty or a stranger or needing clothes or sick or in prison, and did not help you?' He will reply, 'Truly I tell you, whatever you did not do for one of the least of these, you did not do for me.' Then they will go away to eternal punishment, but the righteous to eternal life." - Matthew

- "For even the Son of Man did not come to be served, but to serve, and to give his life as a ransom for many." - Mark

- "For the Son of Man came to seek and to save the lost." - Luke

- "For God so loved the world that he gave his one and only Son, that whoever believes in him shall not perish but have eternal life. For God did not send his Son into the world to condemn the world, but to save the world through him. Whoever believes in him is not condemned, but whoever does not believe stands condemned already because they have not believed in the name of God's one and only Son. This is the verdict: Light has come into the world, but people loved darkness instead of light because their deeds were evil. Everyone who does evil hates the light, and will not come into the light for fear that their deeds will be exposed. But whoever lives by the truth comes into the light, so that it may be seen plainly that what they have done has been done in the sight of God." - John

- "Jesus said to her, 'I am the resurrection and the life. The one who believes in me will live, even though they die; and whoever lives by believing in me will never die. Do you believe this?'" - John

- "Believe in the Lord Jesus, and you will be saved—you and your household." - Acts

- "But God demonstrates his own love for us in this: While we were still sinners, Christ died for us." - Romans

- "Christ Jesus who died—more than that, who was raised to life—is at the right hand of God and is also interceding for us." - Romans

- "For what I received I passed on to you as of first importance: that Christ died for our sins according to the Scriptures, that he was buried, that he was raised on the third day according to the Scriptures," - 1 Corinthians

- "Christ is the carpenter of life and the cornerstone of creation; the embodiment of the ultimate, irreplicable sacrifice

– perfect love. He relinquished his royalty for humanity. The cost of such loyalty - an innocent lamb's life. While the cost of betrayal was 30 pieces of silver - and a kiss. Judas was just a stand-in, but any of us could have exchanged our chance at salvation for a meal. The consequences of our corruption and the weight of our choices should have doomed us all, yet through the mercy of his hand we were freed from our penalty. We freed Barabbas and killed our King; but the power of the author of life cannot be restrained by death. The Son of man and Lord of all; at the mention of his name, every other will fall." – Hans

22 - Flashback

Yo bro, it's been a long time.
Heard you're up now, it's been a long grind.
Remember when you used to do uni, extra-curricular and still work part time.

At one point man you had three jobs, alongside the masters - eye on the goal, green pastures.
I Swear you didn't miss those shots.
You took all your chances but you didn't have lots.

You learnt that hard work pays off - that's true...
But smart work makes prof.
Sacrificed much, saw the times get tough, but you paid all your dues - didn't care what it cost.

You prayed for some money but you got none,
So you worked for some money and you got some.
I pray that doesn't mean that your faith's gone,
Keep looking up, you gotta stay strong.
Remain grateful, look at what God's done.
Take a look back at where you've come from.

Enjoy the future, you've only got one.
But remember the past like an old song.

Two degrees, but you're still learning.
It doesn't really matter what you're earning.
I know you're rich now so you stopped caring.
Purpose was texting but you kept airing.

Messaged your mind at the times you were working,
Too busy getting it, no time for searching.
Did it for the fam - so next time call if it's urgent…
Verbatim didn't mix up the wording.

Spending in cedis converted from sterling.
Took the long road, there was no way of turning.
No more returning, just make sure you keep on observing, and also
Just keep on emerging, and finding out truth everyday be determined,
And make sure you text back your purpose - it's yearning…
Put your mind into gear,
It's getting late, but there's still time over here.

Trust me. I always knew you had a plan.
And inside that plan, you had to incorporate the virtues and lessons that made you a man,
You'll never be perfect, just do what you can:

The first rule of growth is to change;
Furthest thing from time, proved nothing was the same.

Principle two needs a frame,

Mark your words on the wall they're attached to your name.

Basically, be a man of your word - keep your promise to self and to those who you serve.

And you already know what's third,

It's to work, so we push through the peak for the perks.

I hope you're still going gym properly,

'Cos it's not about the show or the strength or the muscle -

We trained for the goat mentality, the rest was a by-product, that's the reality.

Are what you eat, you're grain of some sort.

You're always swallowing environment,

But balance your diet and maintain your sauce.

I hope these words are inspiring.

Take note of my letter even though you already know this.

There're certain things you didn't notice.

Time is ticking, sure you noticed.

You can always holla me on short notice.

Kind regards,

HD Otis,

Tryna get this Hovis…

23 - Quarter Life Learnings

The majority of people major in being right about trivial things. Only a minority of people major in being right about profound things. Though there is no single right answer to life, there are many truths. The sooner this is accepted, the more liberating the journey is. The purpose of the quest for an answer, gradually turns into a quest for truth (a sentiment many astronomers share). God has made it so. A design which should indirectly convey to us the significance of embracing journey over destination. Even though it is a familiar phrase, it is not widely practised.

We often engage in confirmation bias, where our eyes light up to things that we already believe and are dim to everything else. Lessons we learn will either build or break these biases over time.

Not all lessons are useless lessons. Many are effective for navigating life's labyrinth. Although we cannot uncover as many answers as our stream of consciousness craves, the magnitude of some of the truths revealed are profound enough to satisfy a multitude of questions. Yes, some answers and lessons discovered, will generate even more thoughts and questions. But questions can serve as a powerful catalyst for embarking on a meaningful and adventurous journey, rather than remaining an obstacle. Answers on the other hand, are just the remarkable and scenic views we're blessed with along the way. The following are a few of my most notable views and lessons.

1. At different periods in your life, revisit what you knew or learnt and see if you now understand them differently.
2. Perception is reality.
3. Pay close attention to anything that happens more than once.
4. The love of money is indeed the root of all evil.
5. There are three ways to beat the game: play to win, don't play at all, create a new game.
6. If all warfare is based on deception - definitely don't let your guard down in front of a fool.
7. Most people are waffling.
8. Real intelligence is very scarce.
9. Wisdom is severely undervalued.
10. Money can, in fact, buy happiness - but it can't buy joy.
11. Curiosity can be had, or later found.
12. Think for yourself (to find out what this really means you must think for yourself).
13. Cheap things are expensive.
14. It is more implicitly rewarding to fill up the memory box, than the money box.
15. A good friend is beyond priceless.
16. A great life is defined by how many good stories you have to tell.

17. You can never unsay what's been said - ever.
18. Team building can be a deeply profound experience or a complete waste of time.
19. There is nothing more unstable that you can put your faith in than materialistic things.
20. Avoiding remorse and regret is key to a satisfying life. It gradually becomes the internal measure of success the older you get.
21. If you ever want to see fate at work, watch a game of football. No individual or team ever outplays fate.
22. Hindsight and foresight are the same thing inverted.
23. Very few people genuinely mean it when they say, "ah don't worry about it, it's fine".
24. Thinking can be immensely enjoyable or terribly burdening.
25. Coincidences aren't coincidences.
26. Gratitude brings humility and gives inspiration.
27. Two blessings can come successively; and so can two setbacks.
28. Suspend your assumption just a bit longer.
29. Trust is affordable to maintain; expensive to lose.
30. Hope is the foundation of all well-being.
31. Proverbs and aphorisms are tried and tested truths.
32. Mind how you treat or respond to every person you come across.
33. Mistakes are usually not the end of the world.
34. The older you get, the more you have to lose.
35. Your relationships determine the colour in your life.

36. Adults aren't real, but you only find this out once people start calling you one.
37. Avoid any type of physical injuries in your youth which you may have to live with forever.
38. The most memorable moments and memories are birthed in spontaneity.
39. Fela climbed the stage in his underpants - white ones.
40. Success is hard and failure is also hard. You must choose your hard.
41. Don't give out your word so easily; Be tactful. Keeping your word is a skill.
42. Letting things go is also a skill.
43. Be slow to open up.
44. A genuine prayer is elevating - even for an atheist or agnostic.
45. Being young is vastly enjoyable.
46. It's true that no situation lasts forever; good or bad.
47. A lack of trust or too much trust shortens the lifespan.
48. Be slow to enter a friendship.
49. Kindness travels a fair distance.
50. Patience doesn't have to be agonising.
51. Life is a mental sport, a spiritual quest, and a physical experience.
52. Age is not an excuse.
53. Validation from others is quite unnecessary.
54. Define your core values and let them determine your decisions - you'll become a more effective and efficient decision maker.

55. It's better to vote than not vote.
56. There are so many different alternatives in life, but the path you're on is the path you're meant to be on.
57. Authentic confidence is a performance enhancement drug.
58. Calculate your risks well and have a contingency no matter how small.
59. The search for meaning is most likely the meaning.
60. God is an artist.
61. One minor moment can define a lifetime - good or bad.
62. Nostalgia.
63. There's a reason if life was a shape, it would be a circle.
64. Life is hard.
65. All hardship is relative.
66. God is real.
67. The right words can indeed speak louder than actions.
68. A great memory will serve you well in many areas of life.
69. Always be mindful of the unexpected.
70. When events change, plans should change.
71. Half of the best parts of life are spent reminiscing about the actual best parts.
72. You only ever truly know a couple of people, and only a couple of people ever truly know you.
73. Lying to yourself is a highly dangerous practice.
74. The answer or the root to a complex issue is usually simple.
75. Keep it simple.
76. Confusion is an illustration. There's always a root, and if there's a root, there's a solution.

77. There's a price to pay for success and a price to pay for failure.
78. Pleasure and value are mutually exclusive, and adding value is not always pleasurable.
79. The idea usually seems better than the reality.
80. Never ever get carried away.
81. Stories of struggle eventually become easier to tell on the other side.
82. You can have much wisdom with very little knowledge and much knowledge with very little wisdom.
83. There is no real lesson that is without pain. If you haven't yet felt pain, the lesson isn't yet complete.
84. Hindsight doesn't have to be rare or significant, to qualify as hindsight.
85. Breakups are soul-shaping - whether intimate, or platonic.
86. It comes in handy to major in minor things.
87. Complexity is made up of many layers of simplicity.
88. Celebrate your wins, even the tiny ones. It's a form of rest and motivation.
89. Your mind has reserves you'd never know it had until you really needed them.
90. Nothing can be gained without sacrificing something.
91. The truth hurts now; lies hurt later.
92. You can still sell to someone who wasn't even interested for free.
93. Don't take life too seriously, no one ever makes it out alive.

94. If you prove to be credible or likeable, people will bend their understanding to fit your ideas.
95. People are both the problem and the solution. They can be stellar inspirations and severe disappointments.
96. We all get a different blessing.
97. We need more questions to live than we do answers.
98. Your plans vs life's plans; may the best plan win.
99. We're not necessarily afraid of the unknown, we're just uncomfortable with the known coming to an end.
100. There comes a time you cannot rely on anyone else to pick you up. You must pick yourself up or stay down.
101. Problems are life's gift.
102. Much resilience and strength is needed for the journey ahead.
103. The passing of enough time will fix a lot - but won't fix everything.
104. Everything is bearable.
105. Laughter is fathomless.

24 - Notion Sick: Drink for Thought

How much can you think before your brain bursts?
Before I start speaking, let me sip first.
Feeding my mind, I'm feeding my mind -
They call it having food for thought, but they never mention the thirst.

What's meant to be a blessing, slightly feels like a curse.
Big roadblock, so I slapped it in reverse.

Hope is like a bubble that protects you from the worst.
But fail to prepare and that bubble might burst.
Can't try again so you need to rehearse.
Pass me the mic let me spit this verse.
Pass me the rum let me calm these nerves for this dance called life, call it 'You Got Served'.

Full of ideas, yeah you might call it gluttony.
Lord, forgive me for my sins, I ain't tryna be greedy - but ain't nobody stopping me.
Tryna score goals, no need for the commentary.

It's me against me.

So keep both Hans under the bar if you're spotting me.

Trying to rep these sets so comfortably, but the pain of the weight is part of the discovery.

God gave me a clean heart, but I stained it.

My spirit's not broken, I just sprained it.

It was hard from the start,

Had ache in my heart,

But this bubble called hope, I maintained it.

I get tired of these thoughts, I call it Notion Sick.

But I'm Pushing forward, can't get motion sick.

The storm on the sea's got me ocean sick;

It's a big wave rocking my relation-ships

Stomach feels hungry but my brain's full.

Can't even lie, I'm still grateful.

I came a long way, I didn't drive here, I walked in the cold,

Man I swear it was painful…

But I was tryna stay faithful instead.

Found my soul, but I was losing my head - in this life you don't get what you paid for, you get what Jesus paid for, so how is Phils dead?

I swear down we were short changed,

And since then, man a lot's changed.

A life for a lesson - what an exchange.

I don't understand - someone explain.

Maybe the Elric brothers can.

Pause to ponder…

Epilogue

The world is designed to restrain big dreams past childhood or youth. Art is inspiration, inspiration is hope, and hope is essential. That's why artists both conventional and contemporary are so revered and celebrated. It's also why people pay so much for motivation (it is inspiration).

Our minds find it harder and harder as we go through life to think outside the box, let alone construct elaborate fantasies and stories. So, the ones who can, and do so, are admired. They have hope and they give hope. It is critical that when you possess hope you share much of it. Except sadly now, even something as pure as hope has been turned into a pyramid scheme or worse by some. They commodify it, mass produce something more synthetic for cheap, and resell at an extortionate amount. They do so in the same way pharmaceutical companies take what's natural, mix it with chemicals to create a pill, and then over-price it to people in need of it. How destructive.

Hope is like the drug that keeps us all going. If you lose all hope, you lose all life.

When we gain hope, it should then be our goal to live a life full of stories and exploration - physically, psychologically, and philosophically, because this is evidence. A receipt, which shows we've been here and we've learnt something. Even if that something is a 'useless lesson', which merely serves as a relic or picture on the wall of your own life, still hang that picture up in your life's exhibition, so that someone else might take a glance and be informed, inspired, and have hope.

Appendix 1

Death with a side of Friendship – Extended

Philip comes from the same word philo. Nearer to one extreme of the interpretative spectrum, lies the idea of someone who has a deep, fathomless, and unbreakable bond with the concept, notion, and abstraction of love (for anything life has to offer) even without full or much understanding of it.

Meaning of Philip - lover of horses.

David comes from the Hebrew name Dawid - meaning beloved or dearly loved or favourite.

Appendix 2

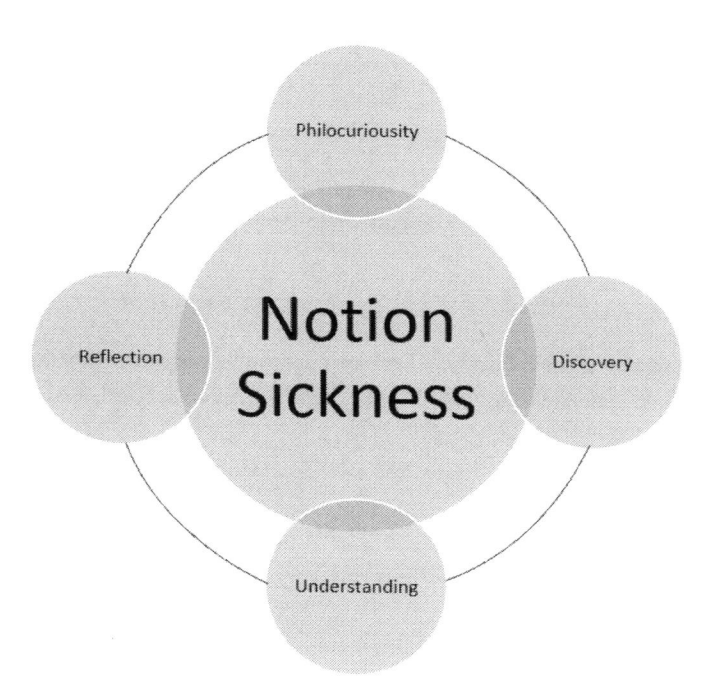

Diagram: A central circle labeled "Notion Sickness" surrounded by four circles labeled "Philocuriousity" (top), "Discovery" (right), "Understanding" (bottom), and "Reflection" (left), all connected by a dashed circle.

The Notion Sick Circle

This figure depicts the active, bi-directional cycle that occurs during notion sickness. Each element surrounding the nucleus is symbolic of the electrons that encircle an atom. Although philocuriousity is a key stimulus, any of these respective concepts can be the starting point of the complete cycle. Each separate idea may also be explored individually, resulting in the partial sensation of notion sickness, rather than its full experience. Notion sickness can have many outer layers beyond its core, which form concentric circles. This resembles a continuous spiral towards, or away from one central point.

Acknowledgements

Friends & Family Hall of Fame: Batch & Some

Vandyke Dodoo & Sue Dodoo

Albert Anane, **David Adjei,** Dwayne Adjei, Edward Elphson, Josh Berritt, Jupiter Gurung, Kaine Wright, Kylron Monah-Macquillin, Louis Aidoo, Miljan Scekic, Nasir Muhammud, **Philip Lamin,** Roman Bhandal, Sima Ali, Stanley Ngagba, Tommy Mayegun, Zyon Hagon, Juliet Lamin, Lester Olusina, Miles Olusina

Get the hoop!

Printed in Great Britain
by Amazon